Manufacturing Management Systems

Manufacturing Management Systems

New Challenges and Profit Opportunities

Edited by

Fred Gruenberger

Produced by

informatics inc

Canoga Park, California 91303

HAYDEN BOOK COMPANY, INC.

Rochelle Park, New Jersey

Library of Congress Cataloging in Publication Data

Main entry under title:

Manufacturing management systems: new challenges and
    profit opportunities.

"Proceedings of a symposium jointly sponsored by
Informatics Inc. and the University of California at
Los Angeles . . . [and] held on the Westwood Campus of
UCLA, March 28-30, 1973 . . . This was the tenth annual
symposium sponsored by Informatics."
    1. Electronic data processing—Production management
—Congresses. I. Gruenberger, Fred Joseph, 1918-
ed. II. Informatics Inc. III. California. Univer-
sity. University at Los Angeles.
TS155.A1M374   658'.05'4   74-4028
ISBN 0-8104-5940-X

1	2	3	4	5	6	7	8	9	PRINTING
74	75	76	77	78	79	80	81	82	YEAR

Foreword

The papers in this volume constitute the Proceedings of a symposium jointly sponsored by Informatics Inc. and the University of California at Los Angeles. This was the tenth annual symposium sponsored by Informatics on a topic of current interest to the information processing community. Previous symposia were:

1964: Disk Files
1965: On-Line Computing Systems
1966: Computer Graphics
1967: Computers and Communications—Toward a Computer Utility
1968: Critical Factors in Data Management
1969: Interactive Computers for Controlling Machines and Influencing People: Setting the Specifications for the Fourth Generation
1970: Expanding Use of Computers in the 70's: Markets—Needs—Technology
1971: Information Systems for Management
1972: Effective vs. Efficient Computing

The tenth symposium, titled "Manufacturing Management Systems: Profit Opportunities and a New Challenge for Computers," was held on the Westwood campus of UCLA, March 28-30, 1973, and was attended by representatives of industry, education, and government.

The speakers at the first nine symposia were almost all computer experts, addressing themselves to topics in the field as seen by those whose business is computing itself. For this symposium, there has been a marked departure: papers were presented by manufacturing management people who use computers as a vital tool toward their goal of improved manufacturing techniques and increased plant efficiency. It is implicit in their theses that computers can be made to do any of the things they wish to accomplish, but they leave it to the computer experts to attend to the details of implementation.

Fred Gruenberger

Preface

The decade of the 1950's has been referred to as the decade of computer technology. It was no minor triumph during the 1950's just to have the computer operate correctly. During the late 1960's, advanced hardware and software systems were developed, with a proliferation of peripheral equipment, compilers, and data base management systems appearing on the market. Thus, the fundamental tools were available to business to achieve significant results from the computer. This current decade, the 1970's, is now being regarded as the decade of applications. The computer and data processing have, at last, come of age.

Over the past 20 years, computerized information processing was considered all too frequently as a "new thing" which had its strong advocates, its chauvinists, and, of course, its detractors. Among these were people who said, "We're spending too much money. . . . We're not getting the value out of the computer. . . . The cost effectiveness of this instrument is not what it should be."

Those days are rapidly ending, and we are entering an age in which there will be enormous payoffs from the use of data processing systems. And it is becoming evident that the most important payoffs will be realized from management information systems that support manufacturing and marketing functions.

Management information systems provide a great challenge to the manufacturing community, as well as to hardware and software practitioners. The advances in modern hardware (especially for large disc file systems) and in software (particularly for data base management systems and compilers) make the challenge well worth accepting.

Such systems are also a challenge to management in that they are difficult to understand. It is a challenge for management to organize the effort properly, to swallow hard and say "yes" to spending money . . . "yes" to spending the time and energy . . . and "yes" to the possibility of upsetting the staff to some degree by installing one of these systems—all because there might be a good payoff.

These new systems are an organizational challenge because they interface primarily with people. They are highly people-subjective and individual-oriented kinds of systems. Computer systems are taking over in areas that were formerly the responsibilities of people, with long years of experience, making subjective decisions on a day-to-day basis that they perhaps did not even realize they were making.

These systems are a challenge because there exists no standard discipline or procedure to implement them within a large and diverse organization. There is a challenge in cost and time, but the payoffs are substantial. Manufacturing control systems can reduce capital requirements and inventory costs and, at the same time, generate a tremendous increase in management effectiveness, production efficiency, and, perhaps, even employee morale.

On a broader scale, an opportunity exists to enhance the cost effectiveness and efficiency of the entire nation with these systems. In competing with foreign countries for the manufacture of goods and the sale of products, our country must rely on its technology. The pocket mini-calculators now available are an excellent example. We could not compete with the old mechanical calculators being imported into the United States because of the low cost of overseas labor, but we could compete with other countries by marketing these new calculators which we were able to develop because of our technological ingenuity. The same possibility exists to improve efficiency and cost effectiveness through the use of the new manufacturing systems and, in doing so, catch up with and even overtake foreign manufacturers, and thereby become competitive in world markets.

Manufacturing is one of the largest enterprises in this country, and the systems discussed at this symposium are, at this time, only in their infancy. We have a long, long way to go, but I think we may be at the knee of the curve and in the next two to three years will see impressive advances in these areas.

Dr. Walter F. Bauer
Chairman and President
Informatics Inc.

Contents

Manufacturing
Management Systems

Information Processing
in Manufacturing:
New Challenges for Management

J. Paul Bergmoser

Vice President, Technical Affairs
Ford Motor Company
Dearborn, Michigan

The printed program for these proceedings listed me as the keynote speaker, and naturally I'm honored at that. But a caveat is in order: I am not a computer expert. The registration forms filled out by the attendees indicate that at least 80 percent of them—and perhaps all of them—know more about computers than I do.

On the other hand, the company I represent is one of the world's foremost consumers of computer services. In addition, those activities of the company I now supervise and those activities that reported to me in my previous assignment together constitute the largest user of computer services within the company. Within those activities, significant improvements have been made in the use of computers in the past few years. Therefore, I would describe my role today as that of a businessman who uses computers extensively in order to make his operations more efficient and profitable.

Before turning to some specific programs within our automotive assembly operations, it might be interesting to point out something about the computers at Ford. We have 416 computers in the company, and on the basis of rental value, we are the fifth largest commercial user of computers in the world.

There are a variety of applications. As you would expect, we put as many of the bookkeeping and administrative tasks on the computers as possible. These programs produce countless reports which are important as management tools.

We have numerous management control programs, affecting every phase of our business. These programs extend from market analysis to the body design engineering department. There, a computer-directed scanner translates the dimensions of the clay models of future products into digital reference coordinates. Further, computerized analytical techniques are used throughout our manufacturing divisions to evaluate alternative production plans.

The most rapid growth has occurred in the use of specialized industrial control computers for testing, controlling, and monitoring different phases of the production process. At our new casting center, for example, a computer controls the metal melting and handling activities, smooths the amount of power required by electric arc furnaces, and calculates the least-cost combination of raw materials. As manpower costs increase and computer costs fall, the computer will yield greater benefits in the years ahead.

Some advances in our automotive assembly operations could not have been possible without the computer. It is appropriate to begin by describing an automobile assembly line.

That may strike you as incongruous, because it would seem that everyone knows about the assembly line by now. But you probably don't think of it the way I do. Your mental picture most likely is that of a frame proceeding down a constantly moving line, with components being added until the finished product is driven away at the end. The depiction seen most frequently is of the body dropping from above onto a chassis near the end of the line.

But for me, the assembly line begins when we place orders for parts with our suppliers. It continues with the shipment of those parts, and gives me the vision of thousands of trucks and railroad cars swarming across the country in all directions from suppliers to our plants. Although people link cars and Detroit, our suppliers are located throughout the country, and our assembly plants are spread from New Jersey to California, and from Minnesota to Georgia.

Next, the parts are funneled toward the assembly line. Now we can go back to the spot where the body drops onto the frame, a dramatic point for the people who tour our plants. Most of them utter a comment something like this: "Isn't it amazing that the colors match?" At the end of this description, I hope you won't think it so amazing, or at least surprising. A lot of us, and our computers, work very hard to make sure the colors match!

The assembly line has another dimension: When the car is driven off the end of the line, it is loaded on a truck or train for shipment to a dealer, and it all ends when a customer drives home in his new car.

I've hinted at an important characteristic of our assembly line. I'm stretching the truth very little to say that the whole system is without warehouses. To be truthful, we can hedge against supply interruptions caused by winter storms or other circumstances, but only for a few days. The constant, programmed flow of parts in our supply line is the essence of the new system I am describing.

I need to make only one more introductory comment, an indication of the size of our supply system. I think I can safely assert that feeding the automotive assembly plants is the largest and most complex problem of logistics in the world. In North America, for example, Ford has 20 car and truck assembly plants which built 2,800,000 cars and 1,000,000 trucks last year. We sell 12 car product lines and 9 truck lines, and within each car line we have different series. And each customer is offered numerous choices of body styles, interior and exterior colors, engine sizes, and optional equipment such as air conditioning, two kinds of radios, and deluxe seat covers, to mention just a few. We could have built those 2,800,000 cars last year so that no two would have been alike.

Those big yearly production numbers mean that we're building several thousand vehicles each day: The record was more than 17,000 units one day last October. A car has an average of 3,000 to 3,500 parts, and we get those parts from about 2,000 suppliers. Ford plants produce some of the major components, such as engines and windshields, but to us an in-company source is much like an outside supply point: The part has to be ordered, shipped, and controlled in the same fashion. On an average day, our plants record 71,000 transactions. And to give you a better idea of what that means, a rail car of batteries received at an assembly plant is one transaction.

There's one other characteristic of auto assembly plants—no longer true at Ford—you may have read about. In the past, when a model run was finished during the summer, the plant was shut down for as long as a month to change over for the start up of production of the new model cars.

Now, in light of what I have just been saying, consider what that means. The spigots controlling the flow of all those parts for the past year's models had to be turned off at just the right time, and then opened again with a flow of parts for the new models precisely in time to accommodate production schedules.

In the plants, the new model production often required installation of new tools and processes and the rearrangement of physical facilities. The new parts had to be put in place to feed the line. Employees often had to be trained for new procedures. And because we always lost at least some employees during a month-long shutdown, we also had to recruit new employees.

What it amounts to is that the assembly process is a lot like a freight train, in that it's hard to get it started but once it's moving it's equally difficult to stop. This is the system we set out to change. We wanted to eliminate the down time—to be able to switch the plant over from building the old model on a Friday to the building of a new model on a Monday. It has taken about 10 years, and we aren't finished yet, but already we've saved millions of dollars in direct costs and produced other benefits which are real even though they cannot be quantified.

Let me describe briefly the previous procedure: Although we used calculators, we had a manual system in what now seems to be those prehistoric days of 1960. I'll describe just one little piece of the information management process of those days and you can easily imagine the rest of the story. After a shipment of parts was unloaded at the receiving dock of an assembly plant, the invoice went to the plant office and was posted manually in large inventory control books. We estimated that 30 percent of Monday's receipts were posted on Monday, 30 percent on Tuesday, 30 percent on Wednesday and the final 10 percent on Thursday. At the same time, we were building cars and using up stocks, and those inventory adjustments were also posted. We sure had to have a lot of faith—that our suppliers would ship on time, and that we had ordered correctly in the first place.

With such archaic records, we took a financial beating. Because we never knew exactly how much stock we had by part number, we often had too much, and at our volume a few percentage points of excess inventory translates into millions of dollars. We estimate that we spend 20 percent of the value of the inventory in holding the material and in moving it around.

It was easy to run short of stock, so we paid handsomely for premium freight and even overtime in the suppliers' plants to cover shortages. On top of all that, we had to face a near panic each summer when we approached the end of a model year. We called it the "balance out." We tried to schedule production to use up the parts we had on hand, but the orders coming in rarely matched up with what was convenient for us to build. And each car is built to an order, and none for open inventory. Sometimes we couldn't fill the orders we had, and were faced with asking the customer to accept a substitute late in the model run.

And when the last car was finally built, we usually had several millions of dollars worth of odds and ends left over. So you can easily see why we had to close the plant for 3 weeks to get ready for the new model.

That was where we were in 1961 when we began to mechanize the control of our supply line. That was 12 years ago, and there was nothing sudden about any of the many improvements that have brought us to our present situation. Actually there were a lot of skinned knuckles and lessons by trial and error, but most important there was a lot of careful, long-term planning which preceded each phase. In fact, this is the keynote in what I have to say: Planning—careful, meticulous planning—is absolutely essential to profitable computerization.

We are fortunate at Ford to have a fine Systems Office staffed by profit-oriented businessmen who do not merely advocate computer systems for the sake of computers, or for the purpose of expanding their own horizons. Instead, their recommendations flow from a policy that says computer systems should assist management in meeting goals, and that computers must meet the cost-benefit test applied to any other capital item.

Equally important, we've had extraordinary cooperation between sales people, engineering, manufacturing, our own supply staff, outside suppliers, and the assembly division. We wouldn't have been successful otherwise, because the new system cuts across divisional lines and has required a shifting of jurisdictions.

We were aware of the risks when we began mechanization, and we studied a number of case histories, including some failures. We concluded that failure of computer systems was most often the failure of management planning. With that in mind, we moved deliberately. Progress was slow in the eyes of some, but in an organization as huge and complex as ours, any change must be evolutionary.

That's why the first phase, the mechanization of records within the plants, took 4 years, from 1961 to 1965. We had to have an accurate record of our plant inventory if we were to have any hope of eliminating down time for model changeover. We got to that point with the computerized Stock Status System, which overnight permitted each plant to tabulate all transactions of the previous day, including stocks consumed in the assembly process, scrappage, and shipments received.

Substantial savings were achieved when we reached that first objective: We had an accurate picture of our inventory, which enabled us to avoid excess stocks and to cut down on shortages, and thereby cut the bill for premium freight. Also, the balance-out process got easier to manage, and we ended up with fewer obsolete parts at the end of a model run.

But it went slowly for a number of reasons. For one thing, the computer enabled us to uncover shortcomings of our system. Transactions were processed into the computer via the key punch process, for example. Errors in parts numbers on transaction documents were repeated by the key punch operators, and the computer would reject the entry. This required an unacceptably high number of manual interventions, and revealed the lack of discipline in our old manual record system. What we really did was prove to ourselves what we had privately suspected, that our records had been approximations.

We had achieved an improvement in time, but not in concept. The plant knew daily where it stood, but from a company view we still didn't have control of the pipeline, and the computers in the plants and the computer in the general office operated on separate programs.

That brought us face to face with the next problem, the need for a company-wide system. A key decision was the familiar one of whether to go to a centralized or decentralized system. We considered the alternatives and went to decentralized distributive processing. We have a company-wide system and all parties have access, but the basic files are prepared at the plant level.

Although refinements and additions to the system are still coming on stream each year, the second phase of our computerization is now in place. This is the system which enabled us to reduce our plant down time, and I would like to tell you some of its most important features.

I've already mentioned that we have a common program for the plants and the general office. The next key ingredient was the development of a single data file for the parts used in two model years of production. Under the old system, remember, we had to clean out the plant, and then build up an inventory of new parts, using a separate computer program for each year. Today, all parts are in one file, regardless of model year designation.

Obviously, this means that as parts for the new model begin to arrive in the summer, we can begin to get them in place for feeding the line while we are still building the old model. If a part is going to be carried over to the new model without change, we no longer give it a new part number, and this has cut in half the total number of parts we track. With about 51,000 end items in the system, this is a vital simplification.

In the plant each night, the computer calculates the entire inventory by part number. It also analyzes the orders on hand, to determine which vehicles can be built, and calculates the optimal production schedule for the next day and subsequent days.

At the beginning of each business day, therefore, the computer gives the plant manager a snapshot of his order condition, his inventory condition, and his best production schedule, with alternatives. This information from each plant—60 million characters in all—is transmitted overnight to our general office in Dearborn.

At the general office, we're using the same program to manage the flow of materials. The central computer keeps track of all orders to suppliers, and of shipments made by suppliers to the plants. If the computer at a plant detects an impending shortage, the plant can determine, through inquiry to the general office, the expected arrival date of any shipments in transit. The nightly transmissions from the plants automatically trigger a notice to expedite shipment if inventory is below a specified level.

Up to this point, I've discussed how we worked out a system to serve our general office, our plants, and our suppliers. It deals mostly with supply systems once our needs are known. The next step was to work backward within our company toward the engineering and design of the parts themselves.

This brought us much closer to the engineering people who authorize production of parts for the new models. In other words, we got into the act much sooner. Now, just as soon as the need for a new part is identified, and long before final authorization, the data concerning the part goes into the engineering computer and is transferred to our file. We follow the development action constantly, getting ready for the time the part will actually enter our system. As I'm sure many of you know, engineers can—and often do—change their minds. With this system, when the number of engineering changes in previously authorized parts begins to jeopardize our schedule, we can call attention to what could be a serious problem in the making. This occurs because we can monitor the entire system, and while each engineering department may be very close to schedule, the cumulative lag hits us when we have to get parts from supplier to plant on schedule.

A second benefit was identification of some new parts that could be changed over at times other than the first day of new model production. There are always certain parts that have to be changed at the start of a new model run, especially appearance items or features that will be in the marketing spotlight. An example would be the two-way tailgates on station wagons which we introduced a few years ago. But an improved radio doesn't have to be inserted on the first day of a model run. In fact, it should go into production as soon as it's ready. It makes sense and saves money to schedule such items for changeover throughout the year.

This is more important than it might seem at first glance. On the face of it, a radio might seem to be just one part, but in the assembly process it may be as many as 100 parts. The new AM/FM stereo radio, for example, includes the receiver, new remote speakers, and improved wiring plus the nuts, bolts, brackets, and all the rest.

By changing to the new radio in May instead of on the first day of production of the new model, we gained in several ways: People who had to learn installation of the new radio were doing it while the rest of the system was working at normal efficiency. It helped spread out the training cycle that formerly was concentrated on one point in time. On the first day of the new model, the radio people were performing a familiar task. By pulling ahead several hundred parts, and by delaying others, we reduced the workload surrounding the new model launch to a manageable level.

One other piece of background information will help you understand our weekend changeover. Although all car lines have new models each fall, I don't think I'll destroy our advertising effectiveness if I admit that some models are newer than others. What happens is that every 3 or 4 years a car line gets the full redesign treatment—a major change. In other years, it has only minor changes. And that means that most of the parts are carried over.

By the summer of 1971 much of our computerized supply system was in place and we were ready to test its ability to eliminate down time. For this initial effort, we selected plants that were assembling cars due for only minor changes.

How did it work out? I think everybody involved agrees that the launch of our 1972 models, in the late summer of 1971, was the most successful new car launch in our history. We exceeded our own optimistic expectations. Therefore, this past summer, we moved this new system, which we call the back-to-back launch, to all plants building cars with minor changes. We even extended a modified version to some plants building cars with major changes.

We are now able to change over to new models with minor changes during a weekend, instead of closing the plant for 2 weeks. For cars with major changes, we've reduced the down time of between 3 and 4 weeks to as little as 4 days in some cases. Some major changes, however, still require up to 2 weeks. Next summer, we will follow this procedure in additional plants, and we expect to further reduce down time for major change cars.

There are several ways to measure the success. I indicated earlier that we had reduced direct costs by several millions of dollars. But consider some of these other important benefits:

I think any businessman faced with steadily increasing volume would jump at the chance to increase plant capacity without resorting to brick and mortar. Obviously, if we can run our plants for 12 months a year, instead of 11 or 11½ months, we've gained capacity. And we needed it!

I think all of you would agree that you are less efficient on your first day back in the office after vacation. In the old days, we had everyone coming back to work at about the same time, with predictable results. In addition, most of them were coming back to different jobs, in that their functions had changed because of the new models. This meant that we might build only a few cars per hour during the first week, and gradually pick up speed until we achieved the regular rate of perhaps 50 cars an hour.

We've cut that acceleration time, from start-up to full production, to between 1 and 3 days now, down from 15 days only a few years ago. This not only reduces the average cost per unit, but ensures our dealers a better supply of new cars during the fall introduction period when demand is high.

Although we can't prove it conclusively, we feel we've gained incremental sales from having better availability of new cars in the hands of dealers at new car introduction season. We do know that we are producing more cars and trucks during the peak demand period. For example, production in the third quarter increased from 666,000 in 1970 to 750,000 in 1971, a gain of 13 percent. Production in the third quarter last year rose another 10 percent to 822,000 units.

Results in the fourth quarter have been comparable. We built 1,005,000 vehicles in the final 3 months of 1972, a gain of 16 percent from 1971. Of course, sales volume was growing during that period, but much of the increase must be credited to our ability to build more cars because of the better launch system.

Still another measurement is the times per year the inventory turns over, vital to any firm. Our rate has gone up from 18.4 times per year in 1970 to 21.1 in 1971, to 23 in 1972, a gain of 25 percent in 2 years.

We've done more than just keep the plants running steadily, even though that was our objective and that alone would have been worth the effort. We've also become much more efficient in a number of other ways, and I want to mention a few of them.

Once we got control of our entire supply system, we were able to provide management with a picture each morning of the status of all key factors in the system. After a while, this gave us a reliable historical file, and as you would expect, this in turn led directly to a system that would enable us to predict the future.

In fact, it wasn't long until we were in a position to assist the sales department in the development of sales forecasts. We know that yesterday's business is often a better guide to tomorrow's business than is a sales forecast made 2 weeks ago, especially in the forecasting of parts usage and option installations. Our people and the sales people have jointly developed better forecasting methods which have smoothed out our scheduling and resulted in more timely deliveries to our dealers.

We're also more alert to trends in the marketplace. The boom in air conditioning installations in the early 1960s, as an illustration, caught us short, and it wasn't easy to respond. As with the radio, you might think of the air conditioner as a single component. For us, it is an item that requires different engine sizes, oil cooling lines, motor mounts, fans, instrument panels, and radiators, and it calls for additional parts such as control knobs that would not be used otherwise. Altogether, an air conditioner might call for 150 to 200 different parts produced by as many as 100 different suppliers. An early warning system is essential.

Balancing out production at the end of the model year is also easier because of the predictive systems, enabling management to devote more time to the future model than the past model. The same system enables us to do a better job of ordering parts for the start of the new model year, and to fill up the pipeline with the proper mixture. We're also better off because of improved relations with our suppliers. We've moved from monthly to weekly releases to suppliers, and many of them are tied to our computer. This helps us both to be more efficient because of smoother schedules.

Within the company, we've realigned several functions which formerly were involved in procuring new parts and getting them to the plants. Contacts with suppliers, the placing of new business, and the control of the supply line have been consolidated. The value of having a central point of responsibility is such that we all now wonder why we didn't make this change years ago.

In summary, because we were able to design a computer program which greatly improves our supply system, we have been able to eliminate the need for the disruptive yearly shutdown of our assembly plants. We've made enormous cost savings through the reduction of inventory levels, premium freight due to shortages, and obsolescence. The greater understanding of current business conditions which these systems provide has made us much more efficient and in our judgment has resulted in incremental sales.

We were able to accomplish these objectives because management was determined to find ways to eliminate unnecessary costs and inefficiencies, and because of advances in computer technology. New-generation computers made it possible for us to acquire the computer capacity we needed at a cost we could afford. Better peripheral equipment and new telecommunications systems were placed on line with the faster computers.

As a result, we've improved our performance during the past few years. Our cars are more complex, we've added new car lines, and our sales volume has climbed dramatically. Yet we've been able to deliver new cars with better quality and to deliver them to our dealers faster than before.

And so, in my view the computer and its accompanying technology is one of the greatest management tools yet developed. Dazzling as its achievements may be, however, I would caution against making the use of computers an end in itself. As I noted previously, the key word is "planning." Without it, the computer may end up running your business. With it, the computer may well be the key to new levels of efficiency and profitability—or even the key to survival—in this fast-moving, increasingly competitive, high-cost industrial system in which we operate these days.

An Emerging Solution: Integrated Manufacturing Management Systems

Robert F. Williams

Associate Professor
California Polytechnic State University
San Luis Obispo, California

The conventional Material Requirements Planning Technique makes an explosion of the time-phased Master Schedule one level at a time. During each one-level explosion the requirements generated at the lower level are time-offset by an amount intended to represent the time required to produce the higher level of the product. The procedure starts with the highest level in the product structure. By convention, the highest level is generally known as the 0 level. Working with one level at a time, requirements are netted against inventory and lot-sized before being exploded to the next lower level. Eventually, the lowest level is reached, consisting solely of purchased items such as raw material. The result is a time-phased schedule of requirements for all levels of all products appearing on the Master Schedule.

Figure 1 shows a hypothetical product A with its components and their level codes. Note that component F has a level code of 3 because of its structure position on the lower branch. Some of its requirements are generated when level 1 is exploded and some during the explosion of level 2. Not all items on the Master Schedule may be level 0; for example, replacement parts sold to customers are end (Master Schedule) items but may have a level code of 3 or 4. Some components may be used on several end products. In the assignment of level codes, each component must be coded according to its lowest level throughout the product line, so that the requirements from all higher levels as well as possible sales as a spare can be aggregated at one time.

Often the product structure as viewed by the product designer is entirely different from that of the manufacturing engineer. Figure 2 shows a product structure as seen by Production and the same structure as seen by Product Engineering. Care must be taken to assure that the Bill of Materials is correct before it is used for

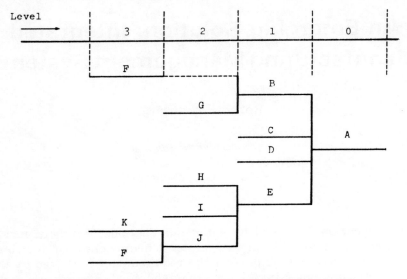

Figure 1. An example of a structure for article A, indicating the components on different lowest levels.

Material Requirements Planning. Some Bill of Materials Processors will produce both an Engineering Bill and a Production Bill. When, in the explosion process, a component is not at the next lower level, but is one or two levels further down the product structure, a provision must be made to hold the explosion information until the program reaches the appropriate level.

After the requirements at one level are calculated by the explosion process, these requirements are "netted" by subtracting the balance on hand and on order from the earliest requirements. After the netting process, all remaining requirements for each component at the current level are lot-sized. After lot sizing we are ready to explode the netted and lot-sized current level into the requirement of the next lower level. Simultaneously, we time-offset each requirement by the production time of the current level.

This procedure is best illustrated with the help of a matrix, as in Fig. 3. The columns in this matrix are time periods and the rows are *articles*, including finished products, subassemblies, components, and raw materials. The arrangement of the articles is such that the level code of every item in the matrix is equal to or less in value than that of all lower items. The Master Schedule requirements of all items are entered in the matrix under the time period during which they are to be shipped (see Fig. 3, A, B, and C). The Requirements Planning Calculation begins by allocating any 0-level components which are in

THE ARTICLE * 3700112 * AND ALL ITS COMPONENTS IN A STRUCTURE TREE

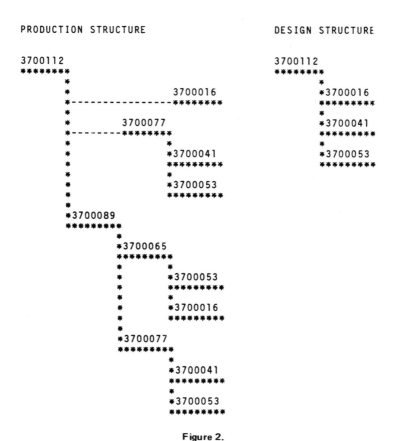

Figure 2.

inventory to satisfy the earliest Master Schedule requirements. After this allocation the remaining "net" requirements are collected into lots according to some optimizing routine. During this lot-sizing procedure the requirements dates are changed. Note that during the lot-sizing, individual period requirements are collected into lots and the requirement date of the lot coincides with the date of the earliest individual period requirement in the lot. Thus requirements are shifted to the left on the time scale during lot sizing. The 0-level requirements are now exploded into requirements at lower levels according to the Bill of Material. The calculated requirements for items with level codes greater in value than 0 are added to their

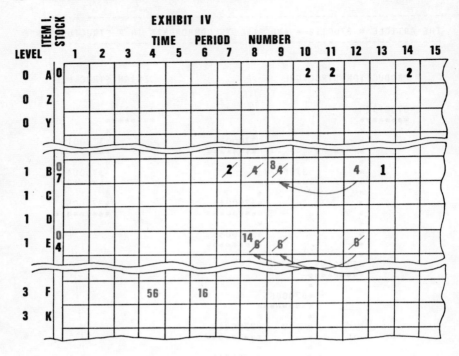

Figure 3.

Master Schedule requirements. The time period in which the addition takes place is time-offset to the left. When all 0-level explosions are completed we are ready to process the products with a level code of 1. The procedure of netting, lot sizing, exploding, and time offsetting is repeated for each level in turn.

Most of the above is straightforward arithmetic. The most critical item in the whole calculation process is the time offset from the higher level to the lower level. Until now we have been calculating material requirements. The same time-offsets and lot-sizing procedures must be used when planning the production operations so that material and capacity are available at the same time. If material is not available, the operation cannot be performed, resulting in three serious and undesirable consequences: (1) Men and machines may be idle waiting for material; (2) delayed performance of operations may result in late deliveries; and (3) uneconomic sequences of operation may be the only alternative to the foregoing.

Since material requirements planning, as usually practiced, makes no attempt to smooth the generated load to fit a finite

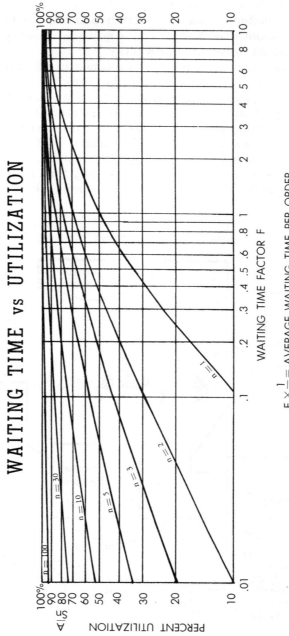

Figure 4.

capacity, overloads and underloads often result. It is thus necessary to include ample queueing or waiting time in the time-offset of both material requirements and production planning so that it will be possible to smooth the load to fit the available capacity and to avoid the undesirable results noted previously.

The inclusion of large waiting times in all time-offsets will reduce to a degree the problems of idle capacity, late deliveries, and uneconomic sequences, but it introduces an undesirable result of its own, namely, a substantial increase in inventory holding costs. The amount of waiting time which must be introduced into the time-offsets is very sensitive to the level of utilization of available capacity which production management is trying to achieve.

Figure 4 shows the relation of waiting time to operation time for various levels of utilization. For example, if it is desired to

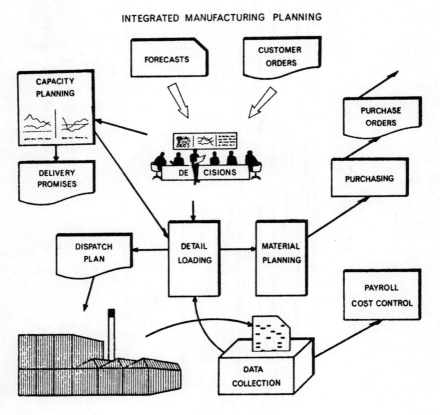

Figure 5.

achieve a utilization of 90 percent of capacity we will need to include waiting time, W, of:

$$W = \frac{A \cdot A}{S(S-A)} = \frac{0.9 \times 0.9}{1(1-.9)} = 8.1 \text{ hours}$$

for each hour of operation time, where A = arrival rate and S = service rate. This is a statistical distribution with a mean of 8.1 hours. Assuming an unskewed distribution, 50 percent of the jobs will wait longer and 50 percent will wait less than 8.1 hours.

This mean has a standard deviation of:

$$\sigma = 8.7 \text{ hours}$$

assuming exponentially distributed interarrival and service times. Thus, in order to attain a confidence level of 84 percent that material will arrive early enough, we should have a time-offset of:

Mean + 1 Standard Deviation = 8.1 + 8.7 = 16.8 hours

for a confidence level of 98 percent, the time-offset must be 25.5 hours for a 1-hour job. This amount does not include time for transportation or inspection required between operations. The time-offset requirements increase rapidly as we attempt to utilize the facilities to more than 90 percent. Inventory holding costs resulting from adequate time offsets in the above procedure can become substantial.

Let us now examine the model of an integrated production/material planning system in which the load is limited to a finite capacity and such that when an operation is smoothed, its material requirements are offset in time by an identical amount—no more, no less. No queueing time is necessary to absorb overloads, as they are not allowed to occur.

To better understand the model let us look at Fig. 5, which is an overview of the Integrated Manufacturing Planning System. It consists of the following system modules:

· *Capacity Planning.* The inputs to this module are Customer Orders and sales Forecasts. This module prepares a Master Schedule and processes customer inquiries, setting feasible delivery dates. Further, it determines long-range needs for production capacity, and initiates the action needed for its acquisition.

· *Detail Machine Loading.* This module loads the Master Schedule on the available production machines. It loads to a finite capacity and determines material requirements, performing netting, lot-sizing, and load smoothing. We shall see later how statistical waiting time-offsets are replaced by deterministic smoothing as required.

· *Material Planning.* Some functions of Material Planning have been integrated into the Detail Loading module in order to avoid the problems discussed earlier in this paper. The Material Planning module handles the production of Purchase Orders, the receipt of materials, calculation of safety times, physical inventory counting, etc.

· *Purchasing.* This module takes care of follow-up on Purchase Orders and vendor files.

· *Dispatching.* This module produces a Dispatch Plan showing the sequence of operations to be performed on each machine and provides other information needed for shop-floor control.

· *Data Collection.* Data is collected on the shop floor concerning the performance of operations and receipt of materials.

· *Cost Control.* Data collected on the shop floor is analyzed to produce performance and cost variance reports.

Figure 6 shows the modules which make up the Integrated System for Manufacturing Planning and its relation to the firm's Total Planning System. We show Corporate Planning at the top of a planning hierarchy. From here plans are originated for New Product development and Market Development. Not shown are the Product Development and Marketing Systems, which are below Corporate Planning in the hierarchy and parallel with Manufacturing in the model.

Within the Manufacturing area the system module which interfaces with corporate planning is an activity known by a variety of names such as Resource Planning, Capacity Planning, or Master Scheduling. We have called this module Capacity Planning, as it deals with acquiring capacity in the long run, to produce the products designed by Product Engineering against orders coming from Markets created by the Marketing Department. In our model, Capacity Planning consists of a simulation system which quickly and economically simulates a hypothetical stream of orders to be produced using actual and/or hypothetical resources. The system identifies imbalances between load and capacity and calculates, for the user, marginal costs associated with various means of curing the imbalance. An important function of capacity planning is the establishment of delivery dates. The two main outputs of this module are a specification of capacity

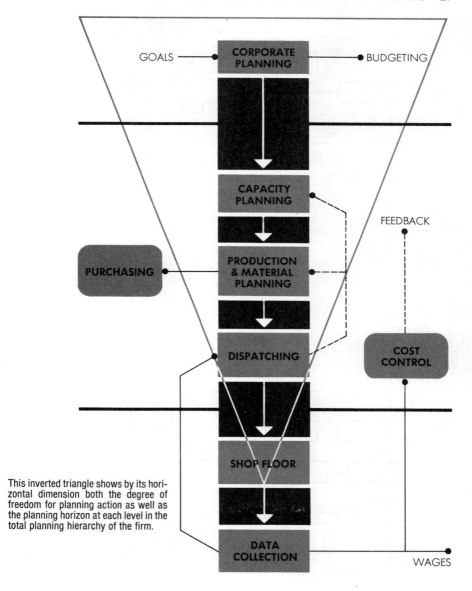

Figure 6. Vertical integration.

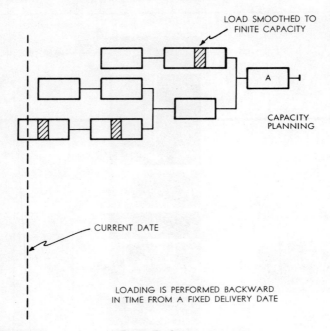

Figure 7. Capacity planning.

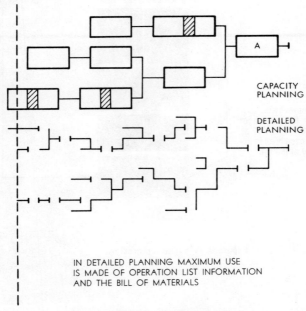

Figure 8. Detailed planning.

types to be available at all future dates within the Planning Horizon and delivery dates of orders.

Figure 6 clearly shows the hierarchical arrangement of the modules. Beneath Capacity Planning lies Production and Material Planning which loads orders and forecasts on the capacity specified by Capacity Planning. The goals of this module are to maximize utilization of the specified capacity, to minimize inventory holding costs, and to avoid late deliveries. Here machine loading and material planning are shown as one integrated module to emphasize the need to coordinate these two activities so that material and capacity meet at the right time and in the right amount. This module outputs a Purchasing Plan and releases jobs for dispatching, satisfying both the goals of the Production and Material Planning module.

The next module is Dispatching, which controls the actions on the shop floor. As work is performed, a Data Collection module captures progress information which it feeds back to the Dispatching module and to a Cost Control module for performance evaluation.

At the top of the planning hierarchy the planning horizon is very long, running to 5, 10, or 15 years. As we move down the hierarchy the planning horizon diminishes until, at the shop floor, we are planning the next jobs to go onto the machines within minutes or hours. As the planning horizon diminishes so does the freedom of choice. Decisions made at a higher level restrict the alternatives available to the lower level. The following discussion will be a detailed examination of the Production and Material Planning module. The explanation will make use of a series of overlays which are reproduced in Figs. 7–14.

Figure 7 represents Capacity Planning of a major order for product A. The shaded areas indicate smoothing that takes place when load exceeds capacity as finite capacity is assumed. The large blocks in the network symbolize aggregated capacity required to produce the order. Capacity requirements are specified by load center and load period. Both load center and load period aggregations are possible. Loading is normally performed from right to left, i.e., backwards in time. For the purpose of ascertaining a feasible delivery date, loading will be from left to right.

At the Detail Planning level, in Fig. 8, work standards and the Bill of Material have become available and are used. Planning is now done operation by operation and machine by machine. Note that in both Capacity Planning and Detail Planning the delivery date is fixed, and production operations are loaded backward in time. That is, the last operation on the final product is the first operation to be loaded. It is loaded in the load period just preceding its delivery date. The loading procedure then loads the next-to-last operation, working back toward time now. (The vertical dashed line on the left signifies the current date.) The last operation to be loaded on any product is the first operation on the lowest level detail.

The capacity available at each load center for each load period has been previously specified by Capacity Planning. As each operation is loaded, the available capacity on the production unit (Load Center) is adjusted as shown in Fig. 9. When the capacity has been exhausted, some other operation will be unable to find capacity in the desired time period. The system then seeks capacity on alternative load centers in the same time period. Failing to find capacity on alternative load centers in the same time period, it moves backward

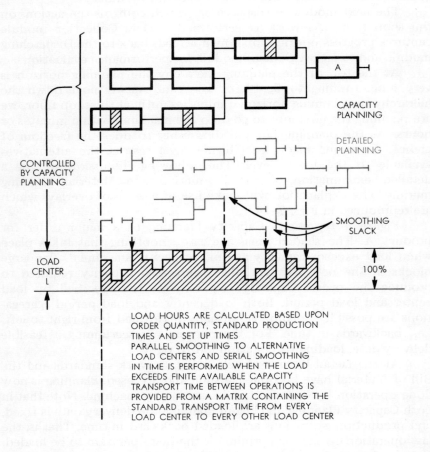

LOAD HOURS ARE CALCULATED BASED UPON ORDER QUANTITY, STANDARD PRODUCTION TIMES AND SET UP TIMES
PARALLEL SMOOTHING TO ALTERNATIVE LOAD CENTERS AND SERIAL SMOOTHING IN TIME IS PERFORMED WHEN THE LOAD EXCEEDS FINITE AVAILABLE CAPACITY
TRANSPORT TIME BETWEEN OPERATIONS IS PROVIDED FROM A MATRIX CONTAINING THE STANDARD TRANSPORT TIME FROM EVERY LOAD CENTER TO EVERY OTHER LOAD CENTER

Figure 9. Capacity reservation.

to the next earlier time period and searches for capacity on the first choice machine and then on alternative machines, in that order, until capacity has been found. Smoothing a job to an alternative machine in the same time period is called Parallel Smoothing; moving to an earlier time period is Serial Smoothing.

Parallel smoothing results in less inventory holding cost than serial smoothing, since the operation is done closer to the delivery date and material is a part of inventory for a shorter period of time. When two jobs require a machine at the same time a special algorithm is used, which will be discussed later. For now we will say only that the algorithm serially smooths to an earlier time period that job which will add the least to inventory holding costs. The breaks in the lines of Fig. 9, representing the product structure, show where serial smoothing has taken place due to the inability of the system to find capacity in the desired time period.

For simplicity, the exhibits show only one major product; in fact, all orders and/or forecasts are loaded at the same time. Orders are held in an open order file which is sorted on delivery date in descending order. We thus start at the end of the planning horizon with the order whose delivery date is farthest in the future. Furthermore, the last operation at the final assembly level is the operation which is loaded first. As we load each time period we consider all operations which can potentially be loaded in that time period. We work backward through time, moving back one time period after having loaded all jobs or used up all capacity. As we move one time period we examine the order file to see if any orders have delivery dates within that time period; if so they become candidates for loading.

As each operation is loaded, the product structure file, where the Bill of Material information resides, is interrogated to see if any materials are required for the operation. If so, a reservation for the required material(s) is recorded in the Product File (see Fig. 10).

At the left side of Fig. 11 is shown how material reservations are netted against any material in stock. In the netting process, a stock-out date, t_0, is established. This is the date when a replenishment order must be on hand. From t_0 we back up (to the left) an amount of time we call Safety Time (see Fig. 12).

Using the Material Requirements Profile in the Product File, a series of Economic Lots across the Planning Horizon are determined. The calculation can be made by dynamic programming, the Carry Even (Part Period) method, the Square Root formula, or any other method. The important point is that we establish not one, but a series of lots. The delivery dates for the economic lot quantities are

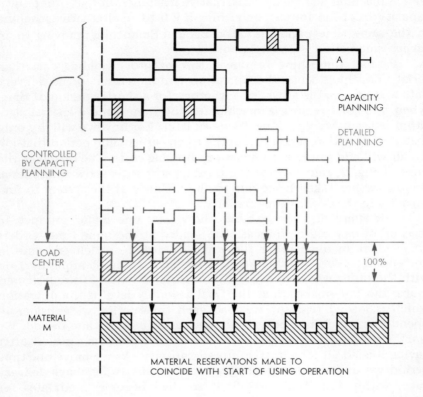

CAPACITY
PLANNING

DETAILED
PLANNING

CONTROLLED
BY CAPACITY
PLANNING

LOAD
CENTER
L

100%

MATERIAL
M

MATERIAL RESERVATIONS MADE TO
COINCIDE WITH START OF USING OPERATION

Figure 10. Material reservation.

established prior to the loading run so that, as the loading is taking place, replenishment orders are loaded simultaneously, as shown in Fig. 13. Load requirements in this model are established deterministically to a finite capacity and no statistical allowance or estimate need be made of waiting times as in the conventional Material Requirement Planning technique. Transport time between operations is contained in a "from–to" matrix which resides in core during the loading run. This insures that the total load, including replenishment orders, is optimally loaded. The replenishment orders, in their turn, produce material reservations.

Stock replenishment order quantities include material reservations lying to the right of (later than) the order's delivery date. Thus,

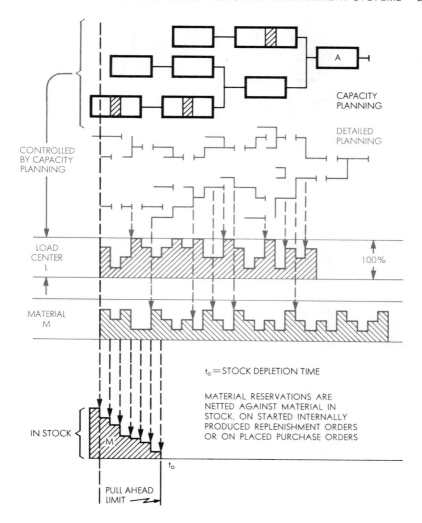

Figure 11. Requirements netting.

when we reach the prespecified delivery date for a replenishment order, the Product File will contain the exact quantity to be included in the order; that is, all material reservations to the right of this order's t_0, and out to the next order in the series.

When the first of a chain of operations on a component falls within the Dispatch Planning Horizon, the whole chain is lifted from the Machine Loading/Material Planning module and released to the

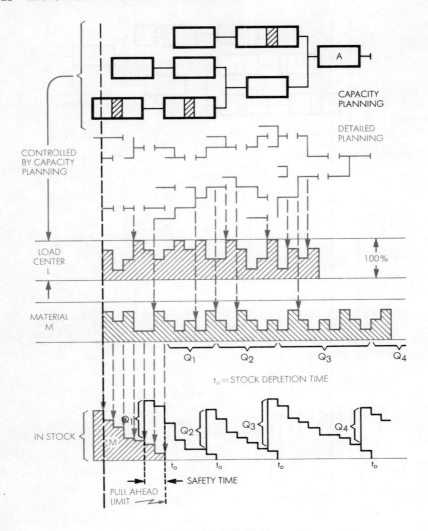

Figure 12. Lot sizing.

Dispatch module (Fig. 14). For this purpose, it is placed in a file called the Current Work File. The jobs in the Current Work File are candidates for the Dispatch Plan, which specifies the sequence in which operations are to succeed each other on the machines.

In the Dispatching module, the goals (objective function) to be optimized no longer include minimizing inventory holding costs. Materials with which this module works must already be on hand as a

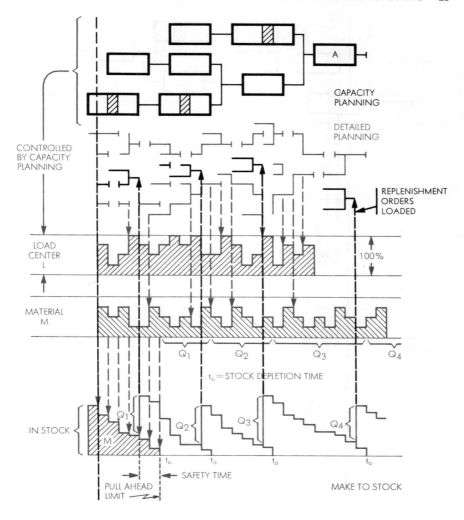

Figure 13.

result of the actions initiated by the Detail Loading/Material Planning module. Dispatching maximizes throughput (utilization), subject to the restriction that delivery dates are to be met.

Figure 15 illustrates two key actions taken in the Dispatching module:

· Overloads are moved to alternative load centers, thus increasing the overall utilization and eliminating potential late deliveries.

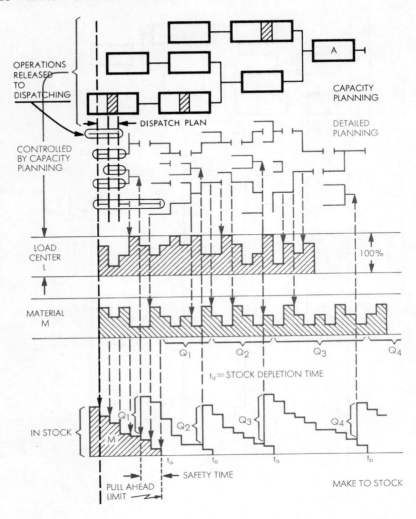

Figure 14.

· When temporarily underloaded load centers persist after the above parallel smoothing, the system looks out over the intermediate term Planning Horizon (e.g., 16 weeks) and searches for candidate operations to be performed now.

Idle capacity (man and/or machine) which is allowed to remain idle is a cost which cannot be recovered. Use of that capacity to

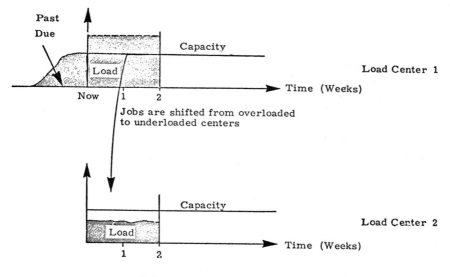

PARALLEL   SMOOTHING   OF   LOADS

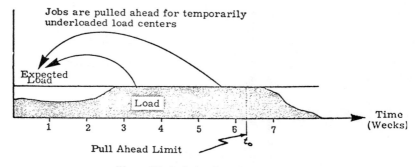

Figure 15. Pull ahead.

perform jobs scheduled for between the near and intermediate term simply puts that capacity in inventory in the form of goods. A rigorous set of conditions must be satisfied if this is to be done properly.

During the inventory netting process of Fig. 11 a stock-out date is established which was designated as t_0. This stock-out date is also specified as the Pull Ahead Limit. Any operation scheduled to be

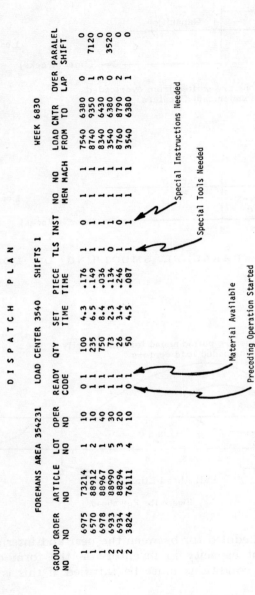

Figure 16.

performed earlier than t_0 can be pulled ahead without changing t_0. It means removing material from stock to work in-process with the traditional crediting of stock accounts and debiting of in-process accounts. This, however, is only an accounting transaction and will not add to inventory holding costs since capital is already tied up in the material. The avoidance of real idle capacity costs can be accomplished without increasing inventory holding costs so long as the Pull Ahead Limit is respected.

In addition to checking availability of material, additional checks are made to see if preceding operations have been performed. Maximum priority, assuming the above conditions are satisfied, is given to operations which are group technologically compatible with other operations planned to be performed in the Dispatching Horizon. Group technology builds run groups of operations, at a machine, which can share set-ups, thereby reducing overall set-up time and thus "creating" additional capacity. More about group technology later.

```
                         L O A D   R E P O R T                        WK 6535

FORM LC  PAST DUE      535 536 537 538 539 540 541 542 543 544 545 546  %  NO
AREA     RE  MIS PREC                                                     MA
             MAT OP

6163 3540 65  20  211 CA  77  77  77  77  77  77  77  77  77  77  77  77 47  2
                      LO  37  70  43  60  28   3  15  62  38   2   4  32
                      MA   3   0   3   0   3   0   3   0   3   0   3   0
                      SU   0   0   0   0   0   0   0   0   0   0   0   0

6172 3679 860 940 534 CA 446 446 446 446 446 446 446 446 446 446 446 446 98 11
                      LO 373 446 432 343 277 406 384 402 446 446 417 410
                      MA   0  18   0   0  18   0   0  18   0  18   0   0
                      SU   0   0   0   0   0   0   0   0   0   0   0   0


         TOTAL   CAPACITY   48657 HOURS
                 LOAD       23204 HOURS    76.7 %
                 LATENESS   14136 HOURS
                 READY       4233 HOURS
                 MIS,MAT     2419 HOURS
                 PREC.OP     7484 HOURS

     VALUE OF IN-PROCESS INVENTORY   1008509




                CA = CAPACITY
                LO = LOAD
                MA = MAINTENANCE
                SU = SUBCONTRACT CAPACITY
                NO MA = NUMBER OF MACHINES
```

Figure 17. Load report.

```
          MISSING MATERIAL REPORT      FOREMAN  PLAN GR  WEEK

          WITH ALTERNATE MATERIALS     354281   3540     6827

**************************************************************
ORDER.NO.           MAT.NO.      NO   KE   IF    QO   DEL.TIME

872-6975321-01      7321453     1o0   1    0    100    6836
                    6932020               500
                    5896291                50
                    3988296               250

872-6975324-01      8891266      50   1    0     50    6828
                    6028991                35
                    7291650               300

864-8887211-01      8887211      68   1    0    200    6825

859-3824663-05      7611129      75   1    0     75    6830
                    3769444               700

**************************************************************
```

```
NO = NUMBER ORDERED
KE = UNIT OF MEASURE
IF = QUANTITY IN STOCK FREE
QO = QUANTITY ON ORDER
```

Figure 18. Missing material report.

```
          O R D E R   S T A T U S   R E P O R T        WEEK 6835

ORDER NO.      LEV  ART.NO.   RE-  INF. OP.NO.  NO.  OP.NO  ORDER  KE
               NO.            ADY  SOU. READY  READY START QUANT.  1

461 711296-02   2   689204     0   PA     0     0     0     68    1
                3   --578211   1   PK          280          272    1
                3   --689208   0   PA    20    72    30      68    2
                3   --478291   0   F                         73    1
                3   --443208   1   PK          210          204    1
                3   --589802   0   PA     0     0     0     136    1
                4   ---339761  0   F                        204    1
                3   --622119   1   F                         68    1
                2   663721     1   PK          140          136    1

521 468236-01   1   468236     1   FO           6            7    1
```

```
PA = ORDERS UNDER PROCESSING
PK = PARKING
F  = WAREHOUSE
FO = FINISHED ORDERS
```

Figure 19. Order status report.

The Dispatching module produces a job sequence for each load center which is based on a set of priority rules, as follows:

1. Operations already started.

2. Any operation whose expected lateness of completion prevents the scheduled start of its subsequent operation.

3. Operations which precede operations at underloaded load centers.

4. Operations which precede operations organized in Run Groups.

5. Operations to which both Priority 3 and Priority 4 apply.

6. All other operations.

Figure 16 shows the appearance of a Dispatch Plan created by the system.

Additional outputs are the Load Report (Fig. 17) and the Missing Materials Report (Fig. 18). The Missing Materials Report lists all materials required for jobs on the Dispatch Plan which are missing. The report shows the order for which the material is needed and the status of any outstanding orders for the missing material. The lines below list substitute materials and their free stock status. Management may request on demand a special report, the Order Status Report (Fig. 19), which gives the status of an order which has been released to the Dispatching module.

Epilogue

When smoothing the load to a finite load center capacity, it is essential to have a smoothing rule which satisfies the objective function of optimum inventory holding costs. The system described in Fig. 20 uses such a rule.

When two jobs compete for the same time on one machine, they can be performed in tandem. Let us call the two jobs A and B. The sequence can be A before B or B before A. The economic consequences are that the material for the first job in the sequence must be ordered early by an amount of time equal to the processing time of the second job in the sequence.

$$\text{Let } T_A = \text{processing time for job A}$$
$$T_B = \text{processing time for job B}$$
$$M_A = \text{material cost for job A}$$
$$M_B = \text{material cost for job B}$$

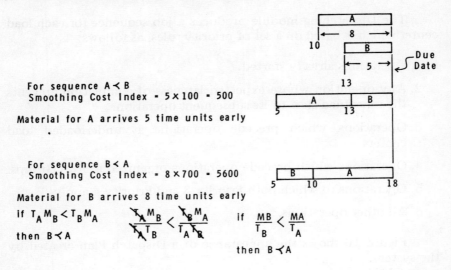

For sequence A ≺ B
Smoothing Cost Index = 5 × 100 = 500

Material for A arrives 5 time units early

For sequence B ≺ A
Smoothing Cost Index = 8 × 700 = 5600

Material for B arrives 8 time units early

if $T_A M_B < T_B M_A$ $\dfrac{T_A M_B}{T_A T_B} < \dfrac{T_B M_A}{T_A T_B}$ if $\dfrac{M_B}{T_B} < \dfrac{M_A}{T_A}$

then B ≺ A

then B ≺ A

Figure 20.

With these symbols we develop a smoothing cost index for each of the alternative sequences such that for the sequence A<B (read A precedes B), the smoothing cost index is $M_A T_B$. The smoothing rule can then be stated that

$$\text{If } \; T_A M_B < T_B M_A, \quad \text{then } \; B<A$$

When more than two jobs compete for capacity on a machine at the same time, this rule becomes unwieldy. To generalize the rule to the multiple job case, divide both sides of the inequality by the product $T_A T_B$ and simplify. This leads to the new rule:

$$\text{If } \; \frac{M_B}{T_B} < \frac{M_A}{T_A}, \quad \text{then } \; B<A$$

This is the smoothing rule used in the Finite Loading procedures of the system.

Note that in Fig. 20 the rate of input of labor, and its recovery at the due date, is not affected by the sequence chosen. It is therefore postulated that: Insofar as the sequencing rule does not cause any of the jobs to be late, labor cost is insensitive to the sequence in which the jobs are performed.

Management Responsibilities in Manufacturing Systems Development

M. L. Golladay

Vice President
Planning Dynamics, Inc.

It is a pleasure to contribute to these proceedings, because they are always a very stimulating, dynamic learning experience which also provide the discipline needed to organize thoughts that have been lying in pieces for some time.

I should emphasize at the outset that my purpose is not to talk as an "expert" on any subject, least of all on computer systems in manufacturing. In recent years, I have had the privilege of working closely with leaders of many different kinds of organizations concerned with developing better concepts, processes, and techniques of management planning. As a result of this—and a continuing review of management literature—I have gained some insights into the thoughts of managers at various levels in organizations with regard to computer systems and their application to modern business life.

My purpose, then, is to offer—in an orderly fashion—what might be called a *digest* of the ideas and opinions currently being discussed by key managers and that hard-to-define group that I will call "computer-management-science-philosophers," as they come to grips with this marvelous new technology.

These ideas are changing rapidly. Many are different from what they were just a year ago and no doubt that process of change will continue. So we are talking about the current state of the art, not the final answers, and, of course, a few points that are of particular importance to me.

Since my subject is obviously too broad to cover in a short time, what I propose is a rather brief overview of three levels of responsibility: top management, manufacturing management, and systems management. The reason for this choice is simply that I feel it's a little dangerous to discuss the responsibilities of manufacturing managers unless they are viewed in relation to their total organizational environment. Can we identify the most important responsibilities of these three management areas? How do they interrelate with each other? Then I'd like to go into a little more depth on what appear to be the three major responsibilities of the manufacturing manager in systems development. Finally, I will consider whether these ideas suggest any areas for possible specific actions which would increase general understanding, technical knowledge, and basic managerial skills and capabilities.

Overview of Management Responsibilities

Within this framework, then, let's try to get a quick overview of some major management responsibilities at three levels in relation to systems development in manufacturing. First, with respect to top management, is a realistic appreciation of the potential results and overall impact of computer systems. This sounds deceptively simple, but in fact it is of growing importance. For years progress has been held back by executives who were afraid of the computer simply because they didn't know how it worked. We seem to be over that hurdle, now that the financial and marketing people have demonstrated that it isn't black magic. The computer is now viewed as a sophisticated tool, and use of it can be delegated to specialists pretty much the same way that you delegate other functions. But now we get a kind of reverse English. While it is not necessary for top management people to be technical experts about computers, this does not eliminate the responsibility for having a real appreciation—in the sense of comprehension—for what a computer can and cannot do. Failure to do this can easily lead to disillusionment when systems can't deliver unrealistically high results, or when the improvement costs more than its worth. As the old saying goes, don't use a $100,000 tool to solve a $1,000 problem. There seems to be general agreement that this kind of understanding is well within the reach of top management.

Second, top management must delegate systems expertise in the operations area to a well-qualified person and see that he has the resources to do the job. This means someone with a "track record" of successful experience in the development/introduction/implementation of computerized systems in manufacturing. Experience to date suggests that the do-it-yourself route is expensive and potentially dangerous when you are talking manufacturing systems applications. The reasons for this are varied but have a lot to do with the impact on the people involved—an important point to be covered later. But a competent systems person isn't enough—true delegation means giving that person the resources required to get the job done. The pages of management are full of well-engineered "bridges" that never reach the other side of the river for lack of resources. Systems take time and money; be sure they are available.

Third, the responsibility is to have a clear policy that the purpose of computer usage is to do things better. In using the computer, let it be a matter of policy that we are not satisfied with simply speeding up what we now do by hand. You don't have to be a systems expert to realize that in manufacturing applications, especially, the computer can measure and analyze and inform us about many operational aspects that are either not feasible by hand or haven't even been thought of. To borrow a phrase from Alvin Toffler, author of *Future Shock* (New York: Random House, 1971), computers should give us "information rich by conscious design." Management should be wary of stacks of papers turned out by high-speed computers. These typically represent the automation of the previous manual system, not a creative, carefully thought out new process of giving us better answers for control and decision-making. The computer has the capability of doing things better than we now do by hand, and that's the way we ought to be using it. And it's a management responsibility to see that this is the way it is thought about throughout the organization.

Finally, there is the responsibility to define objectives and evaluate performance. Keep in mind that computer systems can be designed to do a lot of things, ranging from increasing productivity and saving money to creating jobs that weren't needed before (and even lunch-hour chess games). The point is: In what one or two areas will improvement give you the greatest payoff at a price you are willing to pay? Specify the objectives you want and be sure your system is designed to produce them. The record is already pretty clear on this. Manufacturing systems that have come on stream with reasonable time and cost and have been considered successful were generally in organizations where top management had insisted on the first step, namely, careful planning of the objectives to be achieved by the system, together with meaningful ways to measure those results and evaluate overall performance.

These four areas, then, seem to stand out as being major responsibilities of top management in the development of computer systems in the organization.

Turning to the manufacturing manager, perhaps an obvious point should be made first—which is that he shares in some of the same responsibilities as top management (as do most other key managers in the organization) because he shares in total corporate responsibility. To save time, I will assume that this is apparent and move on to consider three major responsibilities of the manufacturing manager. Since these will be discussed more fully later, here I simply want to identify them as part of this overview of management responsibility.

I would suggest that the three most important responsibilities at the manufacturing managers' level are these:

1. Determining *whether a system is needed* and, if so, seeing to it that the *needed system* gets introduced. I suspect that this may be somewhat controversial ground, but there is a strong argument for saying that the determination that a system is needed and then seeing to it that the proper system is installed is a line responsibility.

2. Formulation of objectives/costs for the system both in the design stage and when it's operating. In meeting both of these objectives, the manufacturing manager will have to depend heavily on information from various specialists in the computer field. But this does not relieve him of the responsibility of seeing to it that the system meets *his* objectives at a price *he* is willing to pay.

3. Seeing to it that management in his area is supportive of the human changes involved. To discharge this responsibility, the manufacturing manager needs first to develop understanding and insight into the types of changes occurring and their effect on people—and the ability to restructure jobs and provide supportive counseling as required.

Before taking a closer look at these responsibilities, let's consider briefly how the area of the systems manager relates to this general framework. This touches on another controversial area. As I have indicated, the consensus in the management field today seems to be that having an appropriate computer system that works effectively is the line manager's responsibility. From this it follows logically that the systems manager is responsible for providing the staff services essential for the carrying out of the line manager's responsibilities, in this case the manufacturing executive. I appreciate that there can be differences about this between honest men of good will. Stripped of emotion, however, it seems to me that the line of reasoning is pretty clear. The systems manager is responsible for the system in the sense of seeing to it that it provides the *type and quality of service* that has been agreed upon as a *management objective*. The manufacturing manager, on the other hand, has the responsibility of seeing to it that the system is an effective part of his overall operating department. If that is a reasonable point of view, then the basic job of the systems manager is to see that the systems requirements of the manufacturing area are fulfilled in a technical way.

To do this, the systems manager appears to have three major responsibilities:

1. To provide the technical know-how required to meet the specified system's objectives. This means that once the specifications for the system have been agreed on by the proper levels of management, the systems manager has an obligation to bring together the necessary technical resources—hardware, processes, and people—that will deliver the goods.

2. He sees to it that there is an interface between the operations people and the computer specialists (e.g., analysts and programmers). There is now and will continue to be a great need for better communication between those who use the output of the system and the technical specialists who see that the system works. The systems manager should be an individual who, in a sense, has a foot in both worlds. Part of the time he wears the hat of a consultant, helping to clarify the technical side to management and the management side to the technical specialists. Computer specialists tend by nature to be more concerned with what the *computer can do* than with the *needs of the user* of the system. Hopefully, the systems manager will be more people-oriented and will tend to identify more with the user of the system.

3. The third responsibility would be seeing that a continuing technical service is provided to maintain the effectiveness of the system. This would, of course, include providing such standard services as technical advice, monitoring, and controls. Probably one of the greatest services he can render is to be a source of creativity and innovation in the organization. Creativity is especially important to systems managers, not only because they are at the forefront of an electronic technology, but because they can have an important influence on the extent to which their organizations become overstructured and hence rigid. Remember, systems inevitably tend to stifle creativity. The systems manager is uniquely qualified to help see that the system does not lock management into rigid, anachronistic habit patterns. He has an important responsibility to see that the computer system is used in such a way that it frees human minds to think more creatively.

Responsibilities of Manufacturing Management

Having looked briefly at some of the major responsibilities of these different levels of management, let's consider the manufacturing manager's responsibilities in a little more depth and try to identify some of the major aspects involved.

Seeing That the Needed System Is Introduced

To repeat, this means first determining whether a system is *justified* and then seeing to it that the particular system developed is the *right one*. This involves a number of things: analysis, evaluation, getting top management approval—and, also very important, gaining the acceptance of the operating people.

The first thing to be said here, I believe, is to start by discussing the idea of manufacturing systems with the people most directly affected—the staff in the operating plant or department. If you want them to accept and use it intelligently, then let them participate in the preliminary feasibility studies. Bring the systems manager/analyst in at this stage, either from the inside or from outside. This process will help avoid the so-called NIH factor—the general resistance to things "not invented here." This process takes time and costs money and there is always a great temptation to skip it, but it is an investment that will come back to you many times. It virtually assures more realistic evaluation and system inputs that would not otherwise have been thought of and it helps get another very important advantage: namely, understanding and approval of those who will be affected by the system.

A second part of this responsibility suggests that the manufacturing manager should head up the systems study himself. He should not try to duck this role just because he is not a systems expert. For one thing, eventually the computer system will be a major factor in his everyday operating life; if he doesn't exercise a leadership role in the planning stages, he has little ground for complaint when it turns out differently than he expected. Equally important, it takes, for the most part, an experienced operating manager to define operational needs and to help identify the specific information required in order for the system to meet those needs. The systems manager, as the technical expert of the study team, then sees that operating needs are translated into appropriate systems technology so that the required data can be collected and processed in the most effective manner.

And finally, don't try to reinvent the wheel. Use the experience of others to avoid expensive mistakes and pitfalls. True, there is no "off-the-shelf" systems package that will work in any manufacturing situation. But there is a growing body of tested concepts, processes and systems components that can be put together—much like building blocks—to build your own system. As nearly as you can, try to use a *basic approach that can be selectively adapted and modified to meet your particular needs,* one which will not "lock you in" to a fixed way of doing things, but which can be readily modified to meet changing conditions.

Having identified/evaluated that a system is needed, the manufacturing manager now needs top management approval. There are two aspects of this that should be emphasized. One has to do with what I'll call "resistance factors"—psychological factors that can block understanding and acceptance of new ideas such as a proposed manufacturing system.

Probably the most common is simply fear of the unknown. We are generally apprehensive about change when the effects on us are not known. To get computer systems accepted topside you have to get them out of the category of being an "unknown." Often, another "resistance factor" is simply that management is comfortable about current results from manufacturing, and the possibility of increasing production efficiency is not as pressing as some other area that needs improvement. This can be a tough situation. About the only way to meet it is to "make them an offer they can't refuse." But that is not easy, either, because manufacturing managers by reputation, tradition, and what-have-you couldn't possibly know anything about computer systems, could they? This is a fairly common management attitude, and one which represents another resistance factor. Added to these, there is the unfortunate publicity that has already been given to manufacturing systems that did not prove out. Management hears over and over again about a company that tried a manufacturing systems approach and it didn't pay off. It was very expensive and it had a lot of problems. Why? Many reasons, I suppose, but mainly because of poor planning and a failure to commit the needed resources—points already emphasized. But that isn't what top management hears. It hears that something was tried and didn't work. So you're stuck with a poor image, and that requires a creative response. If you're serious about getting approval for a systems project, it pays to anticipate such areas of resistance.

To overcome these obstacles, it is essential to regard top management as your "customer," very much as you would if you were trying to sell a systems application in the marketplace. Begin by recognizing the old marketing truism: people don't buy products and services, they buy *benefits*. Talk to management in terms of benefits it needs, not in terms of what you want. Sound simple? Yes, but how often that basic principle is ignored.

There are various benefits that might be highlighted. You should try to zero in on the one that offers the greatest potential improvement for a given amount of investment and effort. Professor George Steiner, of UCLA's Graduate School of Management, has developed an approach to corporate planning which stresses the identification of a set of "strategic factors." These are critical aspects of the overall activity in which even a very small improvement can have a significant impact on overall profitability; in a word, leverage.

Applying that idea to manufacturing, we know one thing management is concerned about in the production area is dollars of cost. What they want to hear about is numbers of dollars saved. Now it happens that manufacturing usually is the prime influence or control over a very large portion of total company resources. And that sounds like it might represent a "strategic factor." So one approach to getting acceptance of systems development might be to show in concrete terms the kind of leverage possible from even a small improvement in how efficiently those manufacturing resources are being used.

As a rough-cut example, suppose you control total resources— inventory, work-in-process, plant and equipment, payroll, etc.—of $30 million. Further assume that manufacturing efficiency is 70 percent. This means that there is a potential for a 30 percent improvement; that is, 30 percent savings on $30 million. Management will probably say, "That's ridiculous. You'll never get a 30 percent improvement in efficiency." And that is probably true. But if we get only 1 percent, it would still be worth $300 thousand—and we certainly expect to get more than a 1 percent improvement. The point of all this is simply that a little creative thinking about leverage and benefits just might lead to a pretty strong sales message.

Just one other thought in connection with the responsibility of getting the needed system introduced. It is very desirable for the manufacturing manager to guide the selection of the systems people who are going to work in the production area. Again, the manufacturing manager needs to be aware that whatever system is implemented is going to have an effect on his department and that this will be determined in part by the type of systems people involved. He should have some standards in mind and be able to pass on whether people meet those standards. He needs to be aware that, generally speaking, computer specialists tend to identify with the computer and its processes, to emphasize logical sequences (and hence be intolerant of operational untidiness), to prefer a pure, clean world of electronic information flow and A+B decision-making. This is neither good nor bad in itself; it is simply a fact. At the same time, to interface with the people involved, you have to be tolerant of the fact that the real world in the manufacturing shop is not made up solely of mathematical logic, completely devoid of emotion and judgmental decision-making. So the manufacturing manager is well advised to try to obtain systems people with enough give-and-take and understanding of human nature to put people and computer systems together with minimum stress.

Formulating the Objectives/Costs of the System both in

the Design Stage and after It Is Operating

This isn't as impossible as it sounds; in fact, it really is just good, common sense management. It doesn't require a computer expert. You "buy" a computer system the same way you buy anything else, intelligently. You decide on the particular benefits you want and what you are willing to pay for them. A technical expert helps you find the product or service that will deliver them.

But the expert isn't much help unless he knows your objectives. There's an old saying in the planning field: "If you don't know where you are going, any road will take you there." The trouble with the computer is, if you don't know where you are going, you'll probably end up somewhere else.

What do we mean by an "objective," anyway? In business planning, an objective is a very important result (or benefit). In any area of business, including systems development, it is essential to distinguish between *results* and *activities*. Activities might be such things as inventory reduction, machine utilization, elimination of routine decision-making, etc. The overall result, on the other hand, is usually increased profitability. At the manufacturing level this probably becomes lower unit costs, which are, of course, achieved by various means or activities. A good objective must satisfy certain specific criteria:

Achievable—can it be done in your particular shop?

Suitable—is it right for your operation? (e.g., unit costs might be reduced 10 percent but there would be union trouble).

Acceptable—are you willing and able to pay what it costs?

Valuable—best buy for the dollar and worth the cost.

Measurable—the best objectives are in quantified form.

Commitment—full determination for achievement (as long as criteria are satisfied).

What I am suggesting here is that before the manufacturing manager can do an effective job of formulating objectives/costs for a manufacturing system, he first has to have a clear idea of what the overall objectives are for his entire operation. And it's difficult to accomplish that if he doesn't have a clear idea of what the overall corporate objectives are. It follows then that the manufacturing manager who is fortunate enough to belong to an organization where there is a company-wide participative planning process is going to stand a much better chance of formulating and implementing the right decisions concerning system development in his area.

The corporate planning process, properly implemented, provides the necessary frame of reference about what kind of results are most important to the company as a whole. This enables the manufacturing head to develop objectives for his department that support the efforts of the total organization and enable him to systematically answer a series of key questions: What result is the manufacturing area trying to achieve? Which of those results are most important? What decisions have to be made in order to achieve those results? Who has to make them? What is the minimum information needed? Where is this information available and what is the *most effective way to collect and process the information* and get it to the individual who needs it to make decisions?

As you view recent experience in the business field, it's hard to escape the conclusion that careful, creative management planning is a key element in making the right decision concerning whether and how to introduce systems, in the manufacturing area in particular. It is unfortunate that so many still think of management planning as taking time away from the job to speculate about the future, whereas the real purpose of management planning is to provide *a better current frame of reference* for the decisions you have to make today.

Providing Needed Support for the Way People
Are Affected by Computer Systems

This was identified as the third major responsibility of the manufacturing manager, and, as suggested earlier, the kind of job that is done here may have a great deal to do with the success or failure of systems application in the manufacturing area. The introduction of computer systems affects people in many ways, and often different people are affected in different ways. I suspect many of us are affected in ways not even fully understood as yet. There are many things that could be talked about here, but let me invite your attention to just four factors which are either more significant than managers appreciate or which may require responses that many managers have not acquired.

The first was already mentioned in another context—that is, fear of the unknown. Now, too often we hear this talked about as "resistance to change." But I would like to suggest to you that it is not change that we are afraid of; in fact, if it were not for the desire to change we would still be living in caves. Actually, people welcome change—when we feel that it will be beneficial to us. We don't resist being given a raise in pay, do we? That is a change, but clearly a beneficial one. It is the uncertainty introduced by certain changes that causes fear and resistance. This means that the computer will be welcome to the extent that is recognized as beneficial and no threat to our well being. To the extent that we are not sure what its effect on us will be, the resulting uncertainty—fear of the unknown—will produce negative and apprehensive reactions.

There are two common failures that help create or magnify this problem. One is inadequate communication. Failure to take time to anticipate the feelings of people; failure to show how the computer system is expected to make production jobs more meaningful; and, of course, failure to do enough *listening* to the other fellow's thoughts and prejudices—in other words, lack of two-way communication. We have to keep in mind that the facts of the situation are not as important as how those facts are perceived; that is, how people feel about them. The other is one I cannot stress too much, which is allowing a sufficient time period for people to make an emotional adjustment to change, especially one as significant as putting in a computer system. Over and over again, management creates its own problems by failing to give people the time they *must* have to "learn to live with" a new and initially uncertain way of doing things: time to think about it, to talk about it, and time to cuss about it a little, too, to drain off emotional feelings. It pays to remember that you cannot change anyone else; you can only create favorable conditions which will make them want to change themselves, that is, when they see that it is clearly in their own interest to do so. And that requires effective communication and adequate time, not to mention insight, patience, and a well-developed sense of humor.

Another factor to keep in mind is the attitude of most production supervisory personnel toward paperwork. Most of them view their primary role as getting maximum output from personnel and equipment. Therefore, they tend to view paperwork, at best, with disdain and more often as a necessary evil. It takes time away from the work that is really important. Management, incidentally, tends to reinforce this attitude by having a rule that production shall not be held up for lack of the written information usually required. This is a clear indication that output is what counts, not efficient "clerical work."

But with the introduction of a computerized system, it isn't long before the supervisor senses that a big change has occurred. Suddenly the boss is relying heavily on the accuracy, completeness, and timeliness of production forms, reports, and other "paper work" generated by his staff. It is not uncommon for supervisors to regard this as a downgrading of their know-how as production experts and a feeling that performance now depends too much on doing something at which they are not experts. Managers have a responsibility to try to identify such reactions in advance and develop knowledge and skills to help people understand and adapt to the changing requirements.

Closely related to this is a third "people" factor—the fact that computer systems tend to erode the psychological importance to people of having exclusive information. Important operating data is now given to the computer, which organizes it and makes it available to anyone who needs to know. This means that no longer can a man maintain his relationship with his boss by serving as a sole source of a particular kind of information. It is a mistake to underestimate the importance of this on organizational relationships. For one thing, having certain information about the job that no one else has forms a kind of "security blanket." Then, too, the authority of everyone in the organization to a large extent depends more on "authority of information" than it does on years of employment or titles given by fiat. It is small wonder that most of us resist giving away something that is so vital to our desire to feel important and needed in the organization. Much of this, I suspect, is unconscious and leads to instances of people devising a kind of special code so that they can comply with the system and yet still have authority of information because the boss has to consult them for an interpretation. Generally speaking, such people aren't trying to wreck the system; they are just trying to cope with what appears to be a threatening situation.

The loss of this kind of personal job information also poses a threat to the individual's decision-making role. This can take two forms: he may suffer a feeling of less importance as a decision-maker or he may be afraid that he will not be able to make the new kinds of decisions now required. Both are serious concerns, but the latter is by far the more difficult to deal with effectively. In most cases, the computer system is only going to relieve the individual of routine mathematical-type decisions, thus freeing him for more interesting, creative, and *important* managerial decision. This will be seen as a great opportunity by some. But it can be very frightening to others, and they will need a lot of help which requires a combination of insight, communication, and counseling skills.

That brings us to the final aspect I want to emphasize. As we introduce systems in a manufacturing area, almost without realizing it, we begin to ask a type of question that may be new to old production hands. The question now becomes, not so much what they can do or know how to do, but *how they decide* what to do. I think we should realize that this is a fundamentally different kind of question, and may have effects on people that we have not thought about much. There is a distinct possibility that people may feel we are questioning their rationality, their ability to come to logical conclusions. And isn't that just a little dangerous when we are concerned with production processes and techniques? Some of the best production people in the world cannot give you logical reasons for a lot of things they do. That doesn't mean the logic isn't there; it simply means they arrived at a decision which is logical by a different route—an intuitive feel for the best way. If you take an intuitively brilliant production man and put too much pressure on him to reduce his "art" to A+B logic, you might generate what is known as "paralysis by analysis." At the very least, this is a sensitive area that should be treated with caution. The computer must have hard facts and tight logic, but let's be sure we are not paying too high a price for it.

Some Areas for Possible Action

These, then, seem to me to be some of the major aspects of management responsibility in manufacturing systems development. What does this mean to you if you are involved in this area in your organization? What are some actions that you might want to consider?

First, do you feel that you have enough background knowledge about systems concepts/management techniques? If not, then attending conferences is just what you ought to be doing. In addition, you might want to consider workshop training courses and a program of reference reading. Should you consider using outside services and assistance? Generally speaking, this should always be considered, even if you have good in-house capabilities, because initially the outsider may be able to accomplish certain things that would not be accepted from an insider. There are a few guidelines that should be kept in mind, however. If you are considering having outside people actually put in a system for you, be wary of a predesigned package where all you have to do is put your numbers into it. But someone with a basic approach—made up of tested components that can be modified and adapted to meet your particular requirements—can probably help you get better results in less time with fewer overall dollars. Keep in mind that a consultant's chief value is to help you get innovations accepted (which is always difficult for the insider) and to give you the benefit of the experience (especially the mistakes) of others. This means that he will be chiefly useful to you in helping to "sell" top management and providing valuable advice in the early stages of development.

There may also be a need to sharpen your knowledge of the processes and techniques involved in results-oriented planning of the type referred to earlier. I don't believe it is an exaggeration to say that the management field has made more progress in developing planning techniques in the past 5 years than in any other single area. The inherent nature of systems applications—both their cost and their tendency to get us efficiency rather than effectiveness—has greatly increased the importance of knowing in advance precisely what results we expect to achieve. In addition, a planning process developed in such a way that all the key people can participate in it effectively becomes much more than simply a way of deciding where you want to go and how you want to get there. It becomes a way of managing change. One of the early statements of this appeared in Judson's book, *A Managers' Guide to Making Changes*. He put it this way:

> How much any management achieves the full benefits that can be derived from a change is determined by three independent variables:
>
> · Their skill in identifying and analyzing the objectives of that change, and those problems requiring solutions
>
> · Their skill in devising successful methods to accomplish these objectives and solve these problems
>
> · Their skill in gaining acceptance and support for both the objectives and the methods for their achievement from the people affected by and involved in the change.

These are the three principles that need to be implemented successfully to avoid or eliminate the undesirable effects that change can have on people. To paraphrase an old saying: "The group that plans together stays together."

One final area you might need to consider is expansion of your knowledge of human behavior. Make an effort to get acquainted with the work of behavioral scientists such as Herzberg, Maslow, Likert, Gellerman, Bennis, and McGregor. What is participative management all about, and how does it relate to systems development? Are you up-to-date on motivational theory? What turns people on and what turns them off? "What makes Sammy run?" It is amazing, but you still hear businessmen saying that part of manager's responsibility is to motivate his subordinates. Yet we know that motivation can only come from within each person; all a manager can do is create a favorable environment, which is different in some degree for each of us. In your work, do you emphasize *satisfiers* (achievement, recognition, work satisfaction, responsibility, and advancement)? When present in the right degree, these result in strongly motivated people. Or do you concentrate on eliminating the "negative"; that is, trying to get rid of *dis-satisfiers* (poor administrative policies and supervision, poor recognition, poor advancement, poor work conditions)? At best, eliminating these merely prevents trouble; they do not result in strongly motivated people.

In summary, computer systems offer us a powerful and potentially rewarding tool for increased effectiveness in the manufacturing area. A primary job of management is to see that they serve people effectively.

Suggested Reading

Cantor, Jerry, *Profit-Oriented Manufacturing Systems*. New York: AMA, 1969.

Churchman, C. West, *The Systems Approach*. New York: Delacorte Press, 1968.

Gagne, Robert M., *Psychological Principles in System Development*. New York: Holt, Rinehart and Winston, 1962.

Green, Edward J., "Are You Managing by Objectives or Delusions?," A Monograph on Planning. Pittsburgh: Planning Dynamics, Inc., 1970.

Greenwood, Frank, *Managing the Systems Analysis Function*. New York: AMA, 1968.

Information Technology, Report 537. New York: The Conference Board, 1972.

Judson, Arnold S., *A Manager's Guide to Making Changes*. New York: John Wiley & Sons, Inc., 1966.

Koprowski, Eugene J., "Systems Management as a Creative Process." *Journal of Systems Management*, January, 1971, pp. 9–11.

Rice, Curtis, "Systems Organization and Strategy." *Journal of Systems Management*, November, 1971, pp. 30–33.

Rush, Harold M. F., *Behavioral Science: Concepts and Management Application*, Studies in Personnel Policy (SP 216). New York: The Conference Board, 1969.

Steiner, George A., *Top Management Planning*. New York: The Macmillan Company, 1969.

Human Factors
in Implementing Systems

John R. Van de Water

Van de Water Associates, Inc.
Canoga Park, California

Systems, to be fully effective in any situation where human beings are involved, must be accompanied by a professional managerial way of life. Let me give you an example of what this means.

A Way of Life

Some years ago we had in our UCLA Executive Program an engineering manager of the Automobile Club of Southern California—Joseph Havenner, who passed away on March 5, 1973, and to whose memory this presentation is dedicated. Mr. Havenner eventually rose to the Presidency of that organization. He was a deeply thoughtful leader, and he was always thinking about the realistic improvement of management systems. But he was also constantly aware of the need for motivating people to want to work together to accomplish particular stated goals.

Mr. Havenner was justly proud of the fact that the objectives that had been established for his Auto Club for 1985, set years before, had been reached in 1973. Such an achievement, coupled with the fact that he had built the Club into the largest of its type in the world, with its myriad of services and 1,700,000 members, reflects a deep knowledge of management.

Mr. Havenner used "Management by Objectives," but he cautioned his associates in management development never to mention "management systems" to anyone working for the Club. "Talk about it as the normal, natural, common-sense way of life for any professional manager. If our people suspect that some new 'system' is going to be imposed on them, their backs may go up, and they will then become defensive, and they may start building cushions to protect themselves against accountability." And that's how he made a system become a way of life.

To Joe Havenner, people were far more important than things, but that does not mean that you exclude a system. You *do* have a system, and you make it work by having people participate, understanding how it works, and appreciating both how it relates to them and how it helps their growth toward self-fulfillment as whole and achieving people.

Systems and Human Beings

You cannot make a good omelette from bad eggs. You cannot make a system work with uncooperative people. To make a system work, you must gain mutual understanding and willing cooperation among the people who must live with it.

In contrast, consider a shipyard that decided to go modular. Their attempt to modernize is of national importance, because the United States has been producing 4.5 percent of the world's ship tonnage, whereas Japan has been producing 48.5 percent. This ship construction facility went through a strike that cost them an estimated $1.5 million a week, partly to establish in their union contract the authority to assign multicraft services to individual employees, to get away from the hard-and-fast craft lines that management felt would decrease their effectiveness as a modular shipyard. Yet, as of a number of months later, their system was not working as smoothly as had been anticipated.

A second shipyard in the same general area is launching a new naval or commercial vessel every 45 days. This second yard decided some years ago to place a major emphasis on their human relationships. They began with key interviews throughout their organization. Management solicited the ideas and thinking of people through the use of outside consultants, with no one being quoted directly. All ideas were passed on to top management. No negative views about individual persons were passed on. The aim was to help everybody and hurt nobody. A training and development program for 950 members of management from all levels grew out of this interview phase. When a union sought an election, it was overwhelmingly voted down. By their vote, some 10,000 employees said, in effect, not that they were against the principle of unionism for those who want it, but that, "We trust our company. They listen to us. They include our interests and concerns as they plan their programs."

That yard reportedly reduced its lost time accidents to 1/8 of what they had been the year before. Through the supervisors' sense of participation, they came to see that at each location they did not have just one Safety Director but that every line manager is a safety director, with the specialist in safety serving to advise him in that task. This yard has highly computerized manufacturing operations, but with participation and involvement of people.

People come first, systems follow. And, of course, both are essential if we are to move from mechanical to dynamic organizations.

Testing Human Relations

We should test our human relations programs against expected results, in the following areas:

1. *Productivity*. It is possible to have good human relations and low productivity. But if the productivity is low, it is proper to question whether the human relations program is effective—that is, whether people trust each other and are relating effectively.

2. *Profitability*. We can define high profitability as a satisfactory return on investment, not only for the owners of the business (on their risk capital), but also for the investment of time, energy, and skill by the nonsupervisory employees and their managers. Low profitability for any or all of these contributors can also raise a question of possible poor human relations.

3. *Appreciation of Roles*. Do people understand and appreciate their own roles and the roles of others with whom they interact?

4. *Conceptual and Coordinating Capability*. Does this capability exist among the participants in terms of accomplished results?

5. *Commitment*. Is there a high degree of apparent subjective commitment to the accomplishment of organizational goals on the part of individuals?

6. *Mutual Respect, Trust, and Confidence*. This is the payoff for making systems work.

I suggest that it is worth some soul searching on these points, to evaluate the human side of business and public sector enterprise. The factors listed above are checkpoints along the way.

"The Next Play"

In one of our recent leadership conferences, John Wooden of UCLA addressed the group. I am sure you'll agree that he is one of the world's truly great basketball coaches. He said, "Never, in my professional career as a coach, has any player ever heard me say, 'Go out and win the game.' What I tell them is, 'Fellows, make every play perfect!' "

Those are two different motives. One is to be at least one point ahead at the end of the game. It often leads to excessive tension and brash action. The other concerns checking myself as I go along in a thoughtful, disciplined, and alert manner, knowing that I'm doing what is right at the moment with my full attention. The better manager acts from the second motive. He knows his priorities and fully concentrates on the one thing he knows that he should be doing at the particular moment.

The finest of systems may fail if the human factors are not properly handled. An imperfect system can be improved toward optimum effectiveness when skilled individuals are committed and involved.

Principles of Human Relations

I suggest that a number of principles be kept in mind, in order to proceed toward systems improvement and adequacy of human involvement.

The Principle of a Sound Ordering of Values

Of course, we should be concerned with material gain. But in our scale of values, we should place our spiritual values at the top; our moral and ethical values second; our human and social values third; and our material values last. If this ordering of our values were deeply and unequivocally applied and demonstrated in our personal and business lives, we would not be experiencing, as so many of us do, such a negative challenge from our children.

The price we receive is the reward for the services we render. The moral issue is not whether we are out to gain more, or to have higher profitability or productivity. The moral issue is whether we are out to get all we can, and then grudgingly give what we have to, to get it; or whether we are out to give our very best, rightly expecting the gain to follow because of what we have given.

The Principle of Communication as Related to Needs

Let me illustrate this second principle with an example that came up at an overhaul base of one of the major airlines during a management development course in communications.

One of the foremen related that his biggest problem was in trying to communicate new rules and changes in systems to his subordinates. He had noticed that whenever he started to talk about "new rules," the people put up an iron curtain. He gave an illustration, and asked the participants how they would handle it.

At the overhaul base of one of their competitors, he related, a mechanic left a large, steel "safety pin" out of the landing gear of an airplane. As a result, the landing gear retracted and his best friend and fellow worker was crushed to death. To guard against the recurrence of such a tragedy, the safety pin was redesigned so that 2 pins were used, connected by a steel cable, in such a way that it would be impossible to forget its proper application. But the use of the new device had to be explained to all the mechanics concerned. How should this be done?

At this point, another participant said that such an important communication should be eyeball-to-eyeball, with an early explanation of its purpose. So he thought that the proper procedure would be to call the men together and begin by telling them, "Fellows, the company has a new rule for you to learn!"

Another supervisor responded with considerably more empathy. He said he could remember that when he was a nonsupervisory employee, an opening like that would have turned him off immediately. He added that he would handle this situation by first describing the tragic accident that had occurred, and then stating, "Fellows, our company wants to see that this kind of an accident does not happen to any of you men!" Then, he said, he would tell them about the new system.

There's a difference in these two approaches. One way says, "I'm the boss and this is the way it's going to be." The other way asks the employees' needs and desires, then plans to communicate in light of those needs, as the employees see them. If this is done properly, the employees will be eager to hear of the system change. And they will appreciate their employer's concern for their welfare along with his own best interests.

The Principle of Progressive Achievement

This is Maslow's principle of the hierarchy of needs, which says that a person must first satisfy his physiological need to survive. Until that is accomplished, all other needs are unimportant, even security and safety needs. "Man does not live by bread alone—unless there is no bread."

When we know that this basic need is currently satisfied, that we're going to go on living, then we become concerned with security.

And next, we generally become concerned about our relations with others. We want to be accepted by others, and to gain their esteem. Then comes our self-esteem. And finally comes our self-fulfillment, as whole human beings, as we feel that our full potential is being developed and realized.

This hierarchy of progressive achievement is not always and for everyone in this order. But the concept helps us to understand personal and situational differences in our inner motivations, to which we now turn.

The Principle of Personal and Situational Differences

The way we lead another individual depends on the kind of person he is, the particular situation in which we are giving leadership at the moment, and our own makeup as a leader.

Compare the leadership of John Wooden with that of other coaches, when you see them on television. Wooden appears much more calm and relaxed, with his concentration on "the next play." Others are often far more excited and tense.

Which is not to say that every coach should function like Wooden. Take another great coach, Vince Lombardi. They say that one of Lombardi's linemen, when asked about his secret of success as a leader, said: "Well, I think it's because he treats us all the same— Like dogs! When Vince says to sit down, I don't even look for a chair!" Vince Lombardi was certainly a great leader, but he was quite different from John Wooden! And note that he was often dealing with a different type of follower, as well.

Likewise, not only different people, but also different situations, call for different types of leadership. In setting up a new system, it is only natural to get people together to discuss its meaning and implementation. After all, when others' ideas are sought and used, the system will tend to become their property, and they are going to want to make it succeed.

But you can't have group discussions in every situation. When a fire breaks out, autocratic action is called for, and not a committee meeting!

The Principle of Interdependence

Labor, management, and owners are like the three legs of a stool. They need each other. Each group invests in the organization, and each deserves a fair return on its investment. We are obligated to recognize that fact, to take steps to see that each group recognizes the right of the others to a fair return on their investment, and to communicate our steps and accomplishments toward this result.

The Principle of Participation

Let me refer to the findings of Rensis Likert of the Social Science Research Council at the University of Michigan. Dr. Likert found that those organizations which seem to be most successful in establishing business systems that lead to high productivity and high profitability are those which regularly hold two-level meetings and, less often but also regularly, hold three-level meetings throughout their organizations. Such meetings, if well managed, build linking pins between levels, as people actively participate and understand what is going on.

The Principle of Total Responsibility

Consider a government contractor that lost $12 million on one contract, largely due to infighting within the firm that led to an enormous breakdown in relationships. A vice president of engineering was quoted as saying, "It's become so hot around here, with two fair-haired boys fighting for the top position when the old man retires, that I need two tail gunners behind me at all times for protection." The "old man," who was often working over 100 hours a week, eventually dropped dead of a heart attack. Neither of the two contenders got the job; an outsider was brought in. The interesting question is, how did this new man clean up the mess? As he reports it, he applied two fundamental principles. And he turned the large loss position into a profit position which he constantly improved; and the division he headed grew from 7,000 to 21,000 employees.

First, he applied the principle of total responsibility. He expected every manager to work with a primary view to the success of the enterprise as a whole, and he expended his own efforts toward this end.

In reviewing a subordinate's work, he of course looked at how the man performed in his own island. But he also looked at how the man performed in relation to the needs of the entire enterprise, and one measure was the number of men whom the manager recommended for promotion out of his area, in this growing enterprise, into positions of greater responsibility. The point is: does the manager think for the entire organization, or just at how good he looks in his own part of it?

The Principle of Lateral Pressures

The second principle which this executive applied was that of lateral pressures. It is directly applicable to the above-noted situation, where a manager was faced with an internal squabble between two of his subordinates. One of them brings the conflict to this senior manager behind the back of the other individual. The manager insists that the conflict be first and fully dealt with laterally, at the level of the subordinates, to try to get it resolved, before he will become involved in any way. At that level, they should make sure that each understands the viewpoint of the other, to the point where they can and do restate the other's arguments to his satisfaction. There is nothing wrong with conflict. In fact, it is vital to a dynamic organization.

The aim is light, not heat. The issue is what is right, not who is right. If the two people involved can be made to see each other's arguments, and each other's proposed solutions, they may either accept one of these solutions or find a third way that is better than either of their original plans.

But if the two subordinates cannot pool their splintered authority and resolve the conflict at their level, they will eventually return to the manager for action at his level. If so, they should come to him together, rather than separately. Their manager is responsible to higher authority to see that lower-level conflicts are eventually resolved through his own arbitration, if necessary.

The Principle of the Mirror

This calls for every person to examine his own actions before blaming the other man for a failure to make the system operate. Perhaps there has been a failure in communication, and the other man's faulty action is due to misconceptions. It is easy to overlook what the psychologists call projection. When we point the finger of guilt at the other man, we frequently have three fingers pointing back at ourselves. At least we should begin by asking whether the real fault lies in whole or in part with our own actions.

The Principle of Supportive Leadership

When you're evaluating another man, it is often desirable to begin with his good points and commend him for those. If you begin with negatives, he may respond with a defensive attitude. Now, of course, good managing always involves getting around to someone's failures—the places where he needs to improve. But even then, you can handle it in two ways. You can say to your subordinate, "Jim, here's where you're no good!" Or, you can say "Jim, here's where you have a real opportunity for improvement!" One way depreciates him. The other way gives him a lift, and suggests that his superior has confidence in him.

The best example I know of this distinction occurred years ago at the opening dinner for a Kaiser Foundation Hospital management development program. Mr. Eugene Trefethen, then Executive Vice President and now President of Kaiser Industries, was in attendance. A young man asked him, "In all the years you have been with the Kaiser organization, what is the most important thing you've learned about leadership?"

Mr. Trefethen responded: "Let me tell you the story of my life. Henry Kaiser hired me when he was a small businessman. He hired me as a ditch digger. He seemed to think I had potential, because before long I became an assistant foreman. In my first week as an assistant foreman, I made a terrible mistake. The old man was about 30 yards away. He came straight toward me, and I felt cold sweat go down my back. I thought to myself, 'Here goes my job!' " I think it is fair to say that right there and then, in those few seconds, Henry Kaiser's leadership determined whether, today, Mr. Trefethen is a ditch digger or its equivalent, or is as he is—the President of Kaiser Industries.

"As Mr. Kaiser got near to me," Mr. Trefethen added, "I noticed that he had a smile on his face, and a twinkle in his eye. And he said to me, 'Did you learn anything from that?' Did I learn anything from that! He hadn't used my mistake to grind me into the soil. He demonstrated his faith in me, and that out of what I learned from my mistake I could be better off, and our company could be better off."

This was certainly a demonstration of supportive leadership.

The Principle of the Positive Use of Personal Fear

We can talk about this in two ways: fear as it applies to ourselves, and fear as it applies to others. In the first instance, I recall the case of a company president who decided to follow the advice of the experts and move from anxiety, where he did not know the cause, to fear, where he came to know the cause.

The president in question had been sleeping fitfully. But when he screwed up his courage and asked himself, "What am I afraid of?" he wrote, "I'm afraid of going bankrupt;" and a sense of relief, in facing the cause, arose. So he took the next step. He asked himself,

"What is the worst thing that could happen to me, if this fear became an actuality?" And he wrote down, "I could go bankrupt." An even greater sense of peace came over him. He said to himself, "I could live with that, and make a new start in life." The result of his freedom from anxiety was an ability to think and plan creatively, once again.

We are given fear for a purpose: to tune us up to meet the worst and face it squarely. We have mechanisms to deal with fear, whereas anxiety deadens us and makes us ineffective. The only question is, how do we respond to fear? Do we stew in our juice and get ulcers, or do we go out intelligently to meet the object of our fear? That's what I mean by the positive use of personal fear.

The other aspect of fear is in our relations with other people, particularly people who do not want to face responsibility and who want to build cushions for themselves against the system. Take as a simple example the person who is chronically late to work. The proper treatment for such a person may be: "We want you here, we value your services. But you've got to shape up or ship out. If you are late one more time in the next 2 weeks, you're out of a job!" That person is likely to adopt a new pattern of living, through acting on repetitive data input into his brain: "I have to be on time." He has been given due warning, and through fear, the pattern of more disciplined living may become subconscious and automatic. And if the person understands the value of his superior's warning, he will probably thank him for using fear before arbitrarily discharging him. He may also thank him for his new freedom from indiscipline, and from having to make an executive decision about whether to get out of bed in the morning!

The Principles of Creativity, the Self-Image, and

Personal Goal Setting and Accomplishment

The value of creativity is obvious. We need discovery, innovation, the synthesis of ideas, and the mutation of elements in a problem, to find new ways of looking at things.

But beyond that, we need to instill in people an appreciation for their brains, and for the power of the human spirit. Each normal person possesses powers that far surpass the capabilities of the computer. Any such person who holds a low self-image is living a lie, and as a result, what he will give to himself and others will be at a very low level, indeed.

Our self-image is like a thermostat. It controls our comfort zone and our effectiveness range. The only thing more traitorous than a low self-image is a high self-image held in egotistical pride. Kirke-gaard put it this way: Our greatest objective in life should be to become what we really are; and what we are is what our potential is.

We should all have a very high self-image, held in humble gratitude for what we have been given. With that, we tend to bring out the undiscovered gold in the competence and character of other people, helping them to rise to meet their full potential.

Then there is personal goal setting and accomplishment. We need to train people in how they can become self-controlled, toward freeing themselves from confusion and inadequacy, by repetitive data input in their minds on the key goals that they want for their entire lives: for personal development, for their family life, for their social life, for their community service life, and for their business and professional life. For all five areas, people should be goal-oriented. I would suggest that such goals should be written out, put to memory, and regularly revised, so that opportunities will be recognized and barriers will tend to be avoided.

Yet of utmost importance is the need for balanced goal orienta-tion, because excellence in clarification of business goals, alone, may lead to disaster. Hence it was reported that in an automobile manu-facturing company after World War II, even though they had achieved tremendous goal-orientation among their middle manage-ment people, their business goals were not balanced with the other areas of their lives, and the resulting divorce rate among those managers was staggering. They had to rethink their values as an organization.

With realistic and balanced goals, clearly stated as positive images of his potential, an individual will tend to be drawn toward their accomplishment as if by a system of mental magnets.

The Principle of Participative Goal Setting and

Accomplishment within the Organization

Management must measure their intended and accomplished results. But before they can properly evaluate achievements they must determine, at all levels and with horizontal and vertical integra-tion of goals and supporting subgoals, their plan for performance measurement at milestone and final dates for intended achievement. And these goals should be established with the creative initiative and involvement of those who will be accountable for reaching them.

Each individual should have routine goals, such as reduction of downtime in manufacturing, increase in field contact time in sales management, or reduction of cost per invoice in billing. We also need problem solving goals, for those areas where we have not reached a satisfactory level in seeking to achieve past goals. But then we need improvement goals, to go beyond satisfactory levels to new standards of excellence. Most often forgotten, we need goals in the area of creative change, so that we move ahead of our competition. And finally, we need an executive council to review constantly our existing goals in the light of changing conditions and opportunities. We must never be satisfied with existing goals, to the point where they become set in concrete.

The Principle of Conceptual Thinking

As an aid toward creativity, goal setting, and accomplishment, we must be able to look at the whole picture and the relation of the individual parts to that whole.

Consider a situation in the petroleum industry where engineers developed a system of automatic loading equipment, to enable truck drivers to do their own loading. The engineers worked out with staff personnel the retraining program for the loaders who were to be displaced. According to the plan, the loaders would not have to take a cut in pay while retraining, and when they were retrained for their new and higher-level jobs, they would move to higher labor grades with higher pay scales.

They had worked out the physical system, and the human system; but there their thinking stopped. They failed to think conceptually about the possible mind set of the people concerned, and the attitude of the union toward new systems.

When the automatic loading equipment was installed, the loaders then saw what had happened to their existing jobs, but without knowledge of the plan for their future. The result was a strike that spread over the entire northern U.S. The union announced that the strike would never end until it was written into contracts that the union had the right to veto any technological change. As it turned out, most of the men on strike did not even know the underlying reason for the strike, which was simply that 10 men had been displaced by a system that would result in their pay increase and would actually increase the workers' security with the improvement of their company's competitive position in the industry.

Eventually the strike was settled, but at enormous cost, both in lost production and in the education program that was necessary to make the issue clear to the employees. Top management did not blame the workers. They recognized that neither the engineers nor the personnel department had thought and planned conceptually, so that people would be ready for the new system before it was installed.

The Secret of Motivation

We have now considered 14 principles in the field of human relations, as related to the effective management of systems improvement. Now let's move to a deeper understanding of our human nature.

You cannot motivate another person. You say, "Nonsense! If I put a gun to your head and tell you to sign a document or I'll shoot you, am I not motivating you?" The answer is, No. You are building a highly influential environment for my motivation from within!

Recall Sir Thomas More, as portrayed in the film and on the stage, in "A Man for All Seasons." His king wanted him to sign a document that was against his fundamental Catholic principles. His family urged him to sign the document, to avoid having his head chopped off. But in effect, Sir Thomas More said: "Look! If I were to sign that document—that expresses a set of values that are totally against everything I believe in—and when I opened my hand, I would not be there!" The very threat that would have motivated nearly anyone else demotivated him from the signing of that document. Motivation depends on the furniture of the individual's mind.

You cannot motivate another person. All you can do is build an environment in which that person can become motivated from within.

The Tests of a Motivational Environment

What are the tests that determine when a manager has produced a sound motivational environment on the job?

1. Do the people who work for us honestly believe that to the fullest extent that their jobs can permit, they will be able to develop their full potential while working for us?

2. Have our people clarified their personal life goals and do they clearly know why they work for us?

3. Do they understand the organizational goals, and were they involved in setting those goals and the means for their accomplishment as they relate directly to their areas of accountability?

4. Is there a recognized, direct relationship between superior performance toward organizational goals and the intrinsic and extrinsic rewards which will help our subordinates achieve their personal goals? Do the best opportunities go to the person with the nice personality? Or are we on a results-oriented basis of rewarding people?

5. Have we established effective management systems for planning, for performance review, for attitude review, and for efficiency improvement?

Motivational Support Systems

Let me single out just one of those systems—performance evaluation. Many view a performance evaluation form as an aid to the expert in diagnosing and curing sickness in people. Many dread a performance evaluation session, as "the time when your boss tells you that you're no good."

But it need not be that way. For example, a manager at the Naval Ordnance Test Station at China Lake, California, related at a recent seminar how much he enjoyed the evaluation sessions with his superior.

In the first place, he said, they were always on time. And they came in two parts. In the first part, his superior asked him to review his own performance for the past year, against the goals which he had been fully involved in setting. Then his superior would comment, and draw his personal conclusions. In the second part, he was asked to set forth the goals he had tentatively prepared for the coming year, and his superior then questioned him to make sure that they were both realistic and sufficiently challenging.

As he put it, "When I have an annual performance review, do I do my homework! I do almost all of the talking!"

This is the way it should be. The subordinate manager spends 100 percent of his time with himself. His superior spends far less of his own time with him. And if the relationship has been properly handled during the year, this will be seen as simply one, vital step in his superior's frank, honest, and open attempt to help his subordinate manager be a maximum success on his job.

Dual Reward Systems

These are the principles that should be applied to making this management system work. They should aim at meaningful goals, self-managed where possible, under developmental supervision.

As noted above, the rewards should be both extrinsic (such as promotions and pay increases), and intrinsic (made available by the superior wherever merited, but accomplished by the subordinate through his own competence and initiative—such as gaining increased experience and new areas of expertise).

As our behavioral scientists tell us, we should effectively employ both highly motivating factors, such as the opportunity for achievement and recognition, and this growth in experience and responsibility, and the low motivational, maintenance factors, such as adequate pay, proper working conditions, good supervisory-subordinate relationships, and job security.

If the low motivational, maintenance factors are not present, there tends to be great dissatisfaction. If they are present, they tend to cause mild satisfaction. If the motivating factors are not present, they tend to cause mild dissatisfaction. If they are present, they lead to extreme satisfaction, and the subordinate tends to come alive within his work environment.

The Meaning of Job Enrichment

It is important to free the individual from undue controls while retaining accountability. Each individual should be allocated natural units of work if that is at all possible. For example, an assembly line operation in a billing department involving small subunits of work by each employee can be changed to a system in which each billing clerk has complete responsibility for all subunits of the operation, in relation to "her own" group of customers.

Wherever possible, people should find the nature of their work to be challenging, in itself, to the point where they can adequately develop their own growth and their own, individual expertise. We are helping to replace employee vegetablization with employee humanization, as we seek and find ways to help people grow to become what they truly are. For, again, what we truly are is what our potential is.

I'm not talking about job enlargement, where you add more units of the same kind of work. I'm talking about job enrichment. This may be horizontal job enrichment, by adding all subfunctions to assure that an individual is engaged in or is supervising a full, natural unit or area of work.

But it may also involve vertical job enrichment, where demonstrated competence results in the delegation of what the superior's responsibilities were, and the allowance of increased freedom of action and personal credit for independently accomplished projects and functions.

A Contribution to Society

What a difference it makes to an individual, when his true, personal accomplishments are seen throughout the organization as an extension of his own personality, and not simply as appendages which are somewhere lost in the maze of his superior's noteworthy accomplishments!

The end result can not only be the better control, planning, and profitability which the organization is rightly seeking. It can also help put an end to the possible anti-establishment attitude of the individual participant, develop a more enjoyable working atmosphere, and build greater acceptance of the organization's methods, systems, and objectives. Society as a whole may benefit, as professional management produces something freer and more enterprising than we generally see in either free enterprise or public sector enterprise today.

And perhaps this humanization process and improved organizational acceptance shall become two of systems management's finest contributions to society, through the improved application of human factors in the implementation of systems.

Systems Planning Aspects of Manufacturing Information Systems

Victor Azgapetian

EOCOM Corporation
Irvine, California

The word "system" has been misused to the point where it is practically meaningless. Information systems have strongly evident "systems" aspects for just one reason: the whole is more than the sum of its parts. When a major system is broken down into individual blocks, and when each individual block may achieve its desired goals to perfection, there still remains a distinct possibility that the overall system will not work as planned.

Why is this? Mostly it is due to what a person experienced in control theory would call "feedback." Such feedback can introduce instabilities not apparent from the individual blocks of the block diagram. It should be noted that it is practically impossible to build an information system without such feedback, whether overt or covert. The straightforward system block diagram can rarely trace all inputs and the interlinking of those inputs. Usually one such input is derived from some system output, which in effect constitutes a feedback loop. Nor are such feedback loops as evident as links between inputs and outputs. For example, every actual system works only within externally applied constraints, such as resource limitations. If these resource limitations are set by the use of resources in some other part of the system, a covert feedback has been set up and unstable, or even wildly oscillatory, systems can result.

Even more important, from a practical standpoint, is the necessity to avoid the building of an involved complex system to achieve an end that could have been achieved by some simpler system. This is the true definition of the "Rube Goldberg," a spectacularly involved system for achieving a simple end. These things require someone to apply level-headed analysis to the overall problem from a somewhat more distant viewing point. Hence the system aspects.

How does one attack, as a practical matter, the problem of handling these aspects? Most of the trouble lies in the definition of the use to which the system is to be put. It is easy to generalize, to make such statements as, "The system is to be an information system to serve all of Manufacturing." It becomes harder to be somewhat more specific: "The system is to provide immediate knowledge of every item in inventory and its cost and allocation and availability." Neither of these is an ultimate goal or mission assigned to an information system. An ultimate goal will not be a statement as to how inventory will be handled, but rather what was hoped to be accomplished by such handling of inventory. A good ultimate goal is "to achieve fewer than 8 days turnaround time at minimum cost." One system for accomplishing this can be directly compared with another such system, and a figure of merit can be assigned, and the cost of achieving improvements in that figure of merit can be determined.

In fact, one of the indications that a true ultimate goal or mission has been properly defined is a statement of a clear figure of merit which quantifies numerically the success of the overall system. It is amazing how many systems are accepted by default, and how little is known as to whether they achieve the fine promise originally planned for them.

The achievement of a well-stated figure of merit for a system is not an easy task. Those who have worked in the field of auto-matically self-optimizing systems know well how difficult it is to make a figure of merit so well quantified that it can be stated to a computer. Disaster lies ahead for any information system where users with diverse interests expect different results. One of the best ways to avoid such a system is to state in advance a clear figure of merit. Such a figure of merit will flush out differing expectations in a hurry; furthermore, it will provide a chance to settle the differing views *in advance* of starting the actual building of the system, and this is a most valuable feature.

The systems planner can also, given such a figure of merit, go through his system and set aside those parts whose operation is so well known, or so obviously capable of optimization, that their contribution to the figure of merit is clear. This allows him to marshal his forces where they are most needed, and, probably most important of all, it allows the system designer to compare widely varying systems. It should be stated that the figure of merit should be in terms of the user, or of the ultimate use of the system, rather than a description of the system itself, for the very purpose of allowing comparison of widely differing systems.

Systems whose figures of merit differ can be compared on a rational basis through the use of that universal touchstone: the almighty dollar. One is not obliged to accept that system which has the highest figure of merit. Instead, a dollar value can be set on various systems having varying figures of merit, and the equivalent of a curve drawn indicating how much more figure of merit can be bought for each dollar spent on the system.

The words "cost effectiveness" are now misused to the point where "cost effective" is thought to be synonymous with "cheap." It is not. Cost effectiveness is related to the slope of the curve of figure of merit versus cost. The cost effectiveness of any change to a system is the increase in figure of merit that will be obtained for every dollar invested in the change. It is very difficult to evaluate. It would be very difficult, for example, to determine how much the change from brass to bronze rocket launch hold-down bolts would increase the chance of a successful crisp, clear photograph of Mars.

Yet, if resources are limited for this system, or for any system, choices such as this must be made. Before cost effectiveness, the increase in figure of merit for each dollar spent on change, can be determined, it is obvious that the figure of merit itself must be quantified and clearly stated. Even if candidate figures of merit are circulated to users and management, it is surprisingly difficult to determine what is really wanted, what is really needed. Long after some system has been designed, built, and delivered, the commonest complaint heard is always, "All I ever wanted was. . . ." Much of the work of the system designer is in determining this need, rather than doing an excellent design for a loosely determined and perhaps only half-correct need.

What is the underlying true figure of merit for a manufacturing system? Is it productivity? Most output? Hardly. Persons experienced in manufacturing systems know that a maximum output system is extremely expensive, since output can always be forced upward a little bit by a lavish expenditure of money. Should the figure of merit then be most output per dollar cost? Hardly. Such a figure of merit will require lavish investment. Should the figure of merit be the most output per dollar cost per dollar investment? Perhaps, although such a figure of merit will spend recurring costs in order to minimize nonrecurring investment. Perhaps the figure of merit should be most profit, or highest return on investment. Doubt exists here as well. As a matter of plain fact, it is a difficult, involved, complex, frustrating task to find a universally suitable figure of merit for large systems. When the system being maximized is a major manufacturing system, or perhaps an entire manufacturing plant, the problem may not be solvable—at least at the present state of technology. The author was part of a team making several studies of a chemical manufacturing plant in an effort to determine the overall operating figure of merit. Many such plants were found that showed good profit—too good profits. After a few years, the companies vanished. Other companies struggle for years in a near-loss situation, but somehow survive and grow.

The true figure of merit for plants such as these may well be the "survivability," which has not yet been quantified and defined, which may, in turn, be the reason that computers are not yet running manufacturing plants.

The feeling one gets in choosing a figure of merit is that it is continually being patched to satisfy one more conflicting demand, and that as fast as you contain it in one direction, it bulges out in another. It is a primary and very real system task to design a system to suit many users (which should be typical of manufacturing systems) all of whom have different talents to apply to the task of increasing the company's viability.

The question arises, should this—or any ultimate mission—be the concern of the system designer? Are not his objectives considerably more limited? Perhaps. Limiting oneself to small systems and local objectives will result in a series of small victories, but these may well be Pyrrhic victories. Almost all of us have seen well-designed systems that successfully achieve some (limited) figure of merit, and which go into service with a flourish of trumpets, but soon fall into disuse because they do successfully something which nobody really wants. Most persons know that a "Pyrrhic victory" is one that costs the victor more than it is worth. Those more familiar with history will remember that Pyrrhus came to such a victory because he decided that he needed a victory for political purposes at the moment and decided to pick on a small up-country hill tribe, an independent village, then not very well known, called Rome. He obtained his assured victory, but Rome went on to become the civilized world, and he died in ignominy. The parallel is very apt.

Can this entire process be avoided by utilizing the potential of existing systems, and building on them, and assuming that their figure of merit, whatever it is, must be the desired one? There is some value to this approach, but more danger. While one would be foolish to fail to take advantage of an existing well-working foundation, remember that systems which are successful at present are almost invariably characterized by close ties to the immediately available resources, and hence are beginning the downhill slide which occurs in the life cycle of every successful system right after its greatest success. In fact, examination of such system life cycles shows that many highly successful systems may have appeared nowhere near as successful at first. If one is to build a system which is to be successful in the future, it is an obvious truism to state that you must look ahead—or hire somebody who can.

A second and more subtle thing to note is that existing systems are often closely tied to paperwork. They ape (or, as it is called, "automate") systems designed around the flow of paper through an accounting-mail-signature system. Building on an existing system may be holding on to the ghost of past paperwork.

In addition to examining the inputs and outputs, it also pays to examine the basic computer system that goes between. Information systems of the type we are considering fall into three different classes. First, they may be straightforward systems for the storage and regurgitation of information. If no attempts are made to organize or make deductions from this information, basically what you have is a file. Realizing this, comparisons can be made with other types of files on the basis of the cost of the figure of merit of each.

More advanced systems will comprise a trace of operation, for the purpose of reading and controlling status. These "modeling" systems, to be valuable, are often extended to the third type, which involves prediction of the effect of actions that have not yet occurred. This is probably closer to modeling in the classical sense, and, in fact, includes prediction. Some simple forms of this are almost necessary, as in anticipating inventory orders.

It is rare that the trained systems analyst can resist the temptation to include prediction, or, perhaps, the folding-in of formalized past experience in such a model. It is also rare that the systems analyst resists the temptation to believe that time series, or cyclic representations of manufacturing or managerial processes have some innate truth, especially if they are complex enough. But caution is in order; it is a dictum that most business prediction is hogwash.

Foster's dynamic predictions from models are an exception. He can be faulted on many counts, including the operations of his apostles, but his underlying method is correct, simple in concept, and directly applicable to information system control of manufacturing processes. If the opportunity arises to attempt such a model, two pitfalls may be pointed out from the writer's experience. One is that such models are far more sensitive to the constraints on their operation than the actual input. In the writer's experience, the rules setting the limits within which linear operation obtains, or defining different regions of operation, tend to determine the output of a complex system as much as the input and the descriptive parameters. Also, even if such a system is successfully built, to use it effectively one must determine some ultimate mission or figure of merit, with all the troubles previously pointed out. Stated another way, building an accurate model of a system is not in itself a worthwhile goal or mission; nor is the fidelity of such a system a figure of merit for successful use.

In summary, we may give the basic elements of the system aspects of such an information system.

1. We must have a clear goal.

2. That goal must be stated in terms of the ultimate mission, the use to which the overall system is to be put.

3. A quantized figure of merit for the system must be determined.

4. Equally intense care must be given to determine how each required output serves the mission, what inputs are required to yield the necessary information to enable the outputs to be determined, and, given these outputs and inputs, the required internal algorithms.

Then, in addition to the figure of merit, we determine the figure of merit per dollar, to judge between "competing" systems, whether these are actually competing systems from outside vendors, or alternates of the design process. Finally, for each change, we discover the figure of merit increase per additional dollar spent in changing, or, as it used to be called, the cost-effectiveness.

At this point, a few caveats are in order. It is worthwhile to do some sort of simple sensitivity analysis to prevent a knife-edge sensitivity of the entire system stability, and system accuracy, to one or two parameters. Again, it is worth repeating the caution about the invalidity of the simplified block diagram: outputs may be more dependent upon the constraints that determine the regions of operation than upon the inputs. (In fact, this visualization of the process as something that makes progress when buffeted by constraints, as opposed to the visualization of a process as an output determined by shaping input, may be the fundamental difference between the mental processes of businessmen and scientists.)

Somewhere early in the game it is required that you ask yourself, "Do I want a (computer-based) system at all?" There are three counter-indications. One is out-and-out costs: Are you building the world's most ·expensive card file? Many unions made computers worthwhile, but librarians and file clerks have become comparatively cheaper. While I firmly believe that, in the long run, the computer will replace all noncreative, nonpattern-recognition people, we are not yet in "the long run."

A second counter-indication occurs when it is desired to postpone an irreversible decision. This is an occasionally (but rarely) worthwhile practice that can be expensive and can be carried disastrously far. It is a favorite ploy of the bean-counter mentality which leads its company to the brink of hidden disaster and then steps aside.

Third, sometimes the computer should be avoided when its use would require you to work around a genius who cannot, or will not, fit into a computer system. Aside from the fact that this is a dangerous dependency, it merely means that the systems analyst should, in all probability, design a different type of system, suited for the genius (and be prepared for the sudden change when the inevitably shocking loss of the genius occurs).

And, in speaking of computer systems, note that I have said nothing about the actual machinery. That will come out of a consideration of the figure of merit. I can, however, give an unscientific, illogical, highly biased opinion about owning computers. Don't buy a computer. In these days, owning computers is a technical art. I note that small companies rent time, while even the large companies are forming separate companies to own the computers that they will use. I also admit, that when the dollars are on the table, I often bypass my own advice.

Where can you go for help? A sad, although biased evaluation says: almost nowhere. Academic institutes? Not in this field. For some unknown reason, universities, including those pursuing advanced programming and information theory, have given little attention to the useful, overall system. Many skilled individuals exist in this field in universities, but no school, clinic, or body of expertise has emerged, as is the case with programming theory. In general (and, I think, surprisingly) industrial organizations are far more advanced. How about "axes-to-grind" places? Yes, if you are used to dealing with vendors and recognize that an enlightened mutual self-benefit is not necessarily altruism. I have had more success with the large companies seeking to gain my future business, than with individual consultants. How about similar companies? Yes, but with a large grain of salt. Few companies are truly "similar." No matter how well this system appears to work, examine it with a jaundiced eye if the company itself is not prospering in its use.

As to the computer technology part, you must decide in advance whether your business is computers or manufacturing. To say "both" is usually to fool yourself. Many excellent manufacturing managers are excellent programmers. Many data processing experts are thoroughly acquainted with the manufacturing process. But both are careers, and a dual careership will be about as rare as the combination of harbor pilot and surgeon.

If your business is manufacturing, I can give you advice as to the computer technology part. First, stay out of all language and computer system arguments. Insist that all statements be made in terms of results, and let the experts choose the language and machinery that will do the job best. "Speak to me in dollars," is crass, but correct.

Avoid the pitfalls of benchmarking. Benchmarking results are difficult to interpret; it is a job for experienced experts. Write a firm specification for the system you want, in your language, throw in a figure of merit, again in your language, and watch the other people benchmark frantically in order to bid on your specification.

How do you compare nonidentical "canned" systems? Put it on a proposal and counter-proposal basis, just as you do when dealing with other types of vendors. As a matter of fact, it is easier to deal with outside vendors, and carry over your knowledge in such dealings, than it is to deal with an internal group. The best systems devised by internal data processing groups that I have seen have come where these groups could install a new system only after going through the same proposal-pricing-evaluation cycle as is customary for outside vendors.

There are some special precautions for dealing with such internal groups. Allow no patching or changing of the system, especially before delivery. Deliver the specified product first and then consider changing it. If delivering what everyone bid on and accepted on a price basis will be disastrous to the company, and if someone responsible can prove it to you mathematically, the odds are he is lying. When upgrading is done, allow it only within boxes, whose purposes you understand and whose change-in-results can be measured—the figure of merit, again. Allow no change unless it is documented and signed off *first*. No group should be allowed a free hand to "improve" the system at will (and yet this is the rule rather than the exception!). Insist that a sharp record be kept of costs, and furthermore, publish them. If your people will not work under these constraints, let them move to a big company, one of the many where such operations can be routinely concealed.

If sharing operations of a system with other parts of a corporation is to be done, get a clear statement in advance of how the priorities for use will be determined. That clear statement must also include the cost sharing algorithm. Be sure there is a statement as to who bears the cost of improvements, and what will happen if the system suits him, but that you want to improve it. Have in advance a written method for dissolving the partnership.

Finally, look both up and down in estimating your future needs. Be sure your system is capable of graceful expansion. Also, remember the military maxim: that the good systems are those that permit of a graceful retreat.

Fundamentally, what is being said is that any man who has reached an executive position in manufacturing possesses a unique set of talents which can be applied to the procurement and operation of a complex information system for that manufacturing process. Use those talents. Do not jettison them with the misapprehension that you must become a computer expert. A computerized information system is the best first step for talented persons to apply their talents to obtain success. Obtaining new talents is the bonus accrued, not the prerequisite. The only other thing you need is a modicum of good luck, which I wish you.

Computerized Tools for Resource Planning and Materials Management

Michael Lodato

Informatics Inc.
Canoga Park, California

Introduction

The thesis developed in this paper is that effective management does not result from decisions made in the face of problems occurring in the factory, but rather that it results from a series of related decisions that are made over time—in some instances over a long period of time. The contention is that the truly effective manager is the one who prevents more problems than he solves. Up until recently, however, factory managers did not have access to management tools which provided them with the visibility they need to anticipate problems and to make decisions which, if properly implemented, would prevent them from occurring. In this paper we will identify and describe some of the tools which are now becoming available. To set the scene, we will outline the concept of Integrated Manufacturing Planning and Control, and use it as a context for application of the tools to be discussed.

Integrated Manufacturing Planning and Control

Figure 1 views manufacturing management in terms of three planning and control levels (based on length of the planning horizon), their associated functions, and some names currently used to identify management tools for supporting each level.

Plans and decisions which affect the lower levels are made at the long-range management level. Specifically, manufacturing planners analyze the demand for products (firm orders, tentative or proposed orders, and forecasts) based on available and planned capacities and make decisions relating to the following:

- a build plan for the factory;

MANAGEMENT "LEVELS" & TOOLS

HORIZON	FUNCTIONS	TOOLS
LONG RANGE (1 TO 10 YRS)	• RESOURCE MANAGEMENT • MASTER SCHEDULE DEV • DELIVERY DATE SETTING • FORECASTING • NEW PRODUCT PLANNING • LONG LEAD TIME ORDERING	• MASTER PRODUCTION SCHEDULE PLANNING • RESOURCE PLANNING • FORECASTING

INTERMEDIATE RANGE
(1 TO 24 MOS.)
	• DUE DATE PLANNING
	  & CONTROL
	• PURCHASING
	• SHOP ORDER PLANNING
	• INVENTORY
	  MANAGEMENT
		• MATERIAL RQMT PLANNING
		• INVENTORY MANAGEMENT
		• PURCHASING
		• CAPACITY PLANNING
		  (FINITE & INFINITE)

SHORT RANGE (1 TO 15 DAYS)	• ORDER RELEASE • DISPATCHING • RECEIVING • TOOLS & STORES CONTROL • COST CONTROL • PERFORMANCE MEASUREMENT • CAPACITY CONTROL	• SHOP FLOOR CONTROL • OPERATIONS SCHEDULING • DISPATCHING/UNLOADING • COST CONTROL • STORES CONTROL

Figure 1.

. lead time quotations for products;

. promise dates for specific customer orders;

. introduction of new products;

. ordering of long lead time materials and components;

. changes in capacity (factory space, extra shifts, machines, labor force, training, subcontracting, make, or buy) (either up or down);

. inventory policies.

At the intermediate-range management level, plans and decisions are made which affect the short-range level, and progress on long-range plans and decisions is monitored. Specifically, production and inventory planners and controllers analyze the current build plan (master schedule) in relation to current capacity plan and inventory picture (on-hand and on-order) and make decisions about

. adjusting the build plan including altering of promised delivery dates on specific customer orders;

- what items and materials need to be purchased in what lot sizes, and when orders should be placed;

- what production items are needed, in what lot sizes, and when shop orders should be released;

- adjusting capacities over the intermediate horizon (extra shifts, subcontracting, temporary labor force changes, temporary worker reassignment, planned overtime);

- temporary adjustment in inventory policies to stabilize work flow in the factory.

At the short-range management level, decisions are made which affect utilization of resources made available via decisions at the higher levels, and which affect the completion of shop and customer orders defined at the upper levels. In addition, actual progress on plans and decisions made at higher levels is monitored.

Specifically, production and material planners, shop supervisors, and foremen analyze production requirements (what and when) in relation to available capacity (making allowance for breakdowns, worker absences, and other contingencies) and current load on the factory, and then decide on

- what shop orders to release;

- short-range capacity adjustments (overtime, temporary worker reassignment, rush subcontracting);

- changing of shop order due dates;

- dispatching work to each work center;

- assigning priorities to jobs;

- expediting specific orders via shortening of time between operations and adjusting priorities;

- adjusting lot sizes;

- splitting lots;

- use of alternative work centers, routings, and/or materials.

The relationships among these planning levels and their associated functions and decisions are fundamental to the concept of integrated manufacturing planning and control. It is this concept, outlined only briefly above, that is used here to discuss the various management tools for resource planning and material management—those used to support the long- and intermediate-range levels.

Long-Range Management Tools

Most often a company's long-range plans are based on crude information and rough analysis. Yet these plans commit the company to resource levels (men, machines, money, facilities, skills, etc.), product mixes, and sales and inventory policies that constrain more detailed planning at the intermediate- and short-range levels.

In selecting long-range planning tools to work in an integrated planning and control environment, care must be taken to ensure that they help management to develop plans which guide, but do not unduly restrict, decision-making at lower levels. This means that the tools should allow managers to test the impact of various alternatives, to leave room for lower level planners and controllers to react to new information and contingencies, and to incorporate feedback on actual conditions and performance.

Forecasting Future Demand

Analysis of future market conditions and forecasts of future demand are the important inputs upon which resource plans are made. If the forecasted demand cannot be met with existing production capacity and there is not enough time or capital to increase the capacity, then it may be necessary to restrict sales activity, as drastic as this may sound.

Basically, there are two types of forecasting techniques; extrinsic and intrinsic. Extrinsic forecasting involves analysis of external factors such as the social, political, economic, and industrial environments, trends and perceived changes in trends, consumer surveys, competitors' activities, product innovations, etc. to yield a forecast of sales. Intrinsic forecasting involves projecting the pattern of actual past events into the future. Both types of forecasting can be used together as checks against each other to develop forecasts upon which management can base future plans. While forecasting can be aided by computerized tools, it should rarely be done in the absence of human judgment, capability, and experience. There are few, if any, computerized extrinsic forecasting tools commercially available. Several intrinsic forecasting systems are listed in the ICP Quarterly, available from International Computer Programs, Inc.

Resource Planning

Tools are now becoming available which transform demand, in terms of forecasts and orders, into an aggregate production plan and capacity requirements to support the plan. The COPICS Manuals, recently released by IBM, discuss a concept for a Master Production Schedule Planning System which, if implemented, would serve this purpose.

One system that has been in use in several manufacturing establishments for as long as 9 years is the Master Schedule and Resource Planning module of PRODUCTION IV—a complete integrated manufacturing planning and control system offered by Informatics, Inc.

Master Schedule and Resource Planning is a self-contained module which can be installed independently to work with the rest of PRODUCTION IV or other planning and control systems. It is currently assisting managers in

- setting delivery dates;

- establishing after-receipt-of-order lead times;

- developing master production schedules;

- planning the resource requirements for facilities, men, and machines;

- planning the use of overtime, shift work, and subcontracting;

- coordinating engineering, work preparation, and other non-production activities with the making of the product.

Operation of Master Schedule and Resource Planning is based on a set of Standard Load Plans, which define the time-related individual capacity requirements for the manufacture of each product. Orders (definite and tentative) and forecasts, stated in terms of Standard Load Plans, are input along with capacity plans. The system then computes the capacity required for each period and loads it against the planned capacities for the periods.

The loading process performs backward loading of orders and forecasts and forward loading of orders for which delivery date inquiries have been received. From backward loading, a Gross Load Plan is generated including the raw (unsmoothed) load, which is made without regard to capacity constraints and the smoothed load which moves work backward toward "time now" when available capacity is insufficient (see Fig. 2).

If overload conditions persist, work may be shifted into the past. This is an indication to manufacturing planners that there is an imbalance between demand and planned capacities that cannot be resolved easily by shifting work among time periods.

MASTER SCHEDULE AND RESOURCE PLANNING

FACTORY	LOAD CENTER NO.	LOADCENTER NAME	NO. OF MACHINES
S		TOTAL FACTORY	PRODUCT GROUP MM2

NORMAL CAPACITY		EXTRA CAPACITY			EFFECTIVE TOTAL CAPACITY	RESERVED CAPACITY	UNSMOOTHED LOAD		SMOOTHED LOAD		EXTRA CAPACITY REQUIRED	PERIOD
HOURS	MEN	O T HOURS	XTR SHIFT	SUB-CONT			HOURS	MEN	HOURS	MEN		
142080	706		960		143040				2812	12		72 JAN
142080	882		960		143040				4278	23		72 FEB
177600	882		1200		164592				5835	25		72 MAR
142240	883		960		143200				5479	27		72 APR
178000	884		1200		172080				9759	41		72 MAY
142400	884		960		143360				6569	33		72 JUN
178400	886		1200		179600				13406	55		72 JUL
71360	443		480		64704				8714	51		72 AUG
142720	886		960		143680				20797	108		72 SEP
142720	886		960		143680				20374	107		72 OCT
178400	886		1200		172528				33796	146		72 NOV
143040	888		960		162832				30953	146		72 DEC
178800	888		1200		175376				31188	131		73 JAN
143040	888		960		144000				22399	117		73 FEB
143040	888		960		144000				24817	128		73 MAR
143040	888		960		137584				30089	159		73 APR
178800	888		1200		180000				37918	158		73 MAY
143040	888		960		140368				33480	174		73 JUN
178800	888		1200		180000				30998	128		73 JUL
71520	444		480		64848				7278	42		73 AUG
143360	890		960		144320				29502	155		73 SEP
179200	890		1200		174224				31480	134		73 OCT
143360	890		960		144320				21883	113		73 NOV
143360	890		960		137152				18558	103		73 DEC
179200	890		1200		180400				24298	101		74 JAN
143360	890		960		144320				17828	92		74 FEB
143860	890		960		144320				13384	68		74 MAR
143360	890		960		144320				9479	49		74 APR
179200	890		1200		180400				10242	41		74 MAY
143360	890		960		144320				6832	35		74 JUN
179200	890		1200		180400				4210	18		74 JUL
61760	383		480		56064				917	6		74 AUG
143360	890		960		144320				5187	27		74 SEP
179200	890		1200		180400				3794	15		74 OCT
143360	890		960		144320				2702	13		74 NOV
143360	890		960		144320							74 DEC

Figure 2. Portion of gross load plan for a hand welding department.

Backward loading also generates a material requirements file and reports specifying a schedule of nonproduction activities to support the production process.

Forward loading establishes the earliest possible date for future delivery of an anticipated order. The delivery estimation is performed on the basis of the unused capacity remaining after all actual orders have been backloaded, that is, on top of the latest Gross Load Plan. Forward loading is always performed with smoothing.

Because the conditions of periods covered by medium- and long-range capacity decisions are not predictable, Master Schedule and Resource Planning is made flexible enough to allow simulation and experimentation with changes in demand and load center capacities. This "what-if" capability makes it possible to develop an empirical basis for management decisions.

Intermediate-Range Management Tools

Through use of the long-range management tools, production and material planners can be presented with a capacity plan and firm orders and projections of other end-product demand. These planners must now refine the product requirements and adjust the capacity plan so that the best balance can be achieved among the conflicting goals of:

1. high customer service

2. low inventory costs

3. high operating efficiency.

There are very few situations where this task can be accomplished well without the use of computerized tools.

The tools that these planners use must be able to reflect the dynamics of the production process that are implied by the conflicting goals listed above. Fundamentally, the tools are used to assign production capacity to individual end products and customer orders, to review progress, and to reassign capacity as conditions change.

This assignment of production capacity for several months into the future achieves the best results when the load and delivery date requirements are between that which (1) will keep the shop's capacity efficiently utilized on current jobs that are neither far ahead nor behind schedule, and (2) is the highest load and the tightest schedule that can be handled by the shop and still allow for the inevitable rush job from a highly regarded customer, the last minute engineering change or rerun because of scrap losses, and other unpredictable contingencies. If the load and delivery date requirements are below the lower limit, capacity may go unused and/or work may be completed ahead of time and higher inventory holding costs may result. If too much load and unrealistic delivery dates are placed on the shop, work in process will build up, most jobs will fall behind schedule, and almost all work in the shop will have "rush" priorities.

The tools that are used at this level must be able to take a given build plan and a given capacity plan, load the demand against the capacity while keeping track of already committed capacity, and warn of load and delivery date requirements which are outside unacceptable limits. It must be pointed out here that if planners persist in loading a shop well beyond its ability to produce, work will

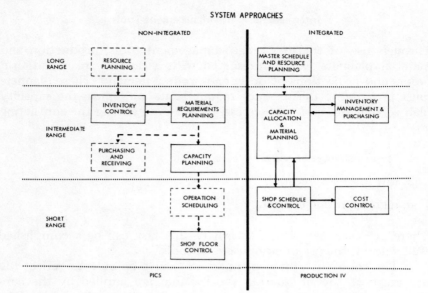

Figure 3.

pile up, shipment dates will be missed, the shop floor will become congested, some capacity will be unused, overtime will be excessive, parts will be missing, overstocks in certain items will result, and there will be heavy use of expediting. Uninformed managers will quickly blame these situations on poor day-to-day shop scheduling and control when the real problem is poor planning at the intermediate level.

There are two basic approaches for configuring tools which support the material and capacity requirements planning and control functions: the nonintegrated serial approach and the integrated approach. The IBM PICS system utilizes the former while Informatics PRODUCTION IV system employs the integrated approach (shown in Fig. 3).

Nonintegrated Approach

The heart of this approach is a set of programs which generate time-phased requirements for piece parts and subassemblies tied to the assembly schedule for final products. The generic term for such a set of programs is Material Requirements Planning, or MRP, for short. The concept of "exploding" bills-of-material back from the date of final product assembly to determine the timing of parts

MATERIAL REQUIREMENTS PLANNING

NON-INTEGRATED APPROACH

PART	ORD QNTY	LEAD TIME	ON ORDER		1	2	3	4	5	6	7	8	9	10
								PERIOD						
PULLMAN SUITCASE	100	1	200	ON HAND	1	2	3	4	5	6	7	8	9	10
PLANNED GROSS REQUIREMENTS					50	100	50	100	50	100	50	100	50	100
ON HAND AND ON ORDER				50		100	100							
PLANNED NET REQUIREMENTS								50	50	100	50	100	50	100
PLANNED ORDERS – DUE								100		100	100	100		100
PLANNED ORDERS – START							100		100	100	100		100	

PART	ORD QNTY	LEAD TIME	ON ORDER		1	2	3	4	5	6	7	8	9	10
								PERIOD						
SUITCASE HANDLES	200	1	0	ON HAND	1	2	3	4	5	6	7	8	9	10
PLANNED GROSS REQUIREMENTS							100		100	100	100	100		100
ON HAND AND ON ORDER				100										
PLANNED NET REQUIREMENTS									100	100	100		100	
PLANNED ORDERS – DUE									200		200			
PLANNED ORDERS – START								200		200				

Figure 4. Material requirements planning—non-integrated approach.

orders manufactured in economic lots has such a high potential for leading to significant business results, that the American Production and Inventory Control Society (APICS) launched a crusade in 1971 to bring MRP to the attention of all manufacturers. Both the non-integrated and the integrated approaches employ this concept. The basic difference between the two lies in the relation of the lead times used and the projected balance or imbalance between demand and capacity available.

In MRP systems, a parts order is placed a standard lead time ahead of the time when assembly is expected to deplete the stock on hand. As shown in Fig. 4, the current supply of suitcase handles is expected to run out during period 3, and the next requirement is for 100 pieces in period 5. To ensure that the assembly of pullman suitcases can proceed as planned (i.e., not be held up because of a shortage of handles), and still allow the standard one-week lead time for suitcase handle-making, an order must be placed during period 4. This replenishment order for an economic lot of 200 units, along with a similar order during period 6, is shown on the figure. Note that each requirement is dictated by requirements at the next highest level. This describes MRP in its simplest form.

It should be noted that the lead times used in MRP are "standard"—i.e., they represent the expected time from order release for the given lot size for the part until it is available to go on to the next highest assembly. Any relationship to capacity availability to meet or shorten that lead time is treated only implicitly. Replenishment orders tend to arrive without regard to the shop's capacity to handle them. The same lead times are used for all such orders until changed by human action. The specification of lead times is a problem that plagues many manufacturers.

To provide management insight into potential capacity problems, Capacity Planning tools have been developed. In the nonintegrated approach, these tools use the due date requirements for build items that result from MRP and load the operations for each item to be built into their appropriate work centers. In this case, standard slack times to account for sending, transporting, receiving, queuing, etc. between operations are used. The sum of slack times set-up and operations times must be consistent with the standard lead times used in MRP. For this and several system and human reasons, the use of these capacity planning tools has not been successful to date.

Capacity planning tools can be used in two ways:

1. subject to capacity limitations

2. without regard to capacity limitations.

In the first case, after a due date has been assigned for each part, standard times for the individual manufacturing operations on the components are loaded in the appropriate work centers, starting with the last or first operation (depending upon whether backward or forward loading is being performed) and allowing for normal material movement and delays. As each job's operating and set-up time is added to a particular work center's load, a check is made to ensure that the addition of the job does not cause the load to exceed the capacity of the work center. If the capacity is exceeded, the job is moved to another time period (earlier with backloading, later with forward loading). If no available capacity can be found within the time required to get the job done on time, either the due date must be changed or capacity adjustments must be made (e.g., overtime, reassignment of manpower, use of alternative work centers, subcontracting). Some of the actions taken—either by the programs or humans—will have an impact on the material requirements developed via the MRP system. This is another drawback of the nonintegrated approach and another reason why the capacity planning system experiences have not been successful.

In the second case—loading without regard to capacity limitations—jobs are loaded (again either backward or forward), using standard move and delay times, and the load is accumulated without consideration given to overloads that may develop. Severe overloads and underloads can be reported to production planners who must then make decisions regarding adjusting of shop capacities to handle the work as loaded and/or to pull work in or push work out to eliminate the overloads.

Integrated Approach to Intermediate-Level Planning and Control

In this approach, loading and the generation of time-phased material requirements are done simultaneously. In this way, planners are presented with material and capacity requirements to manufacture the end products and both sets of requirements are interrelated.

PRODUCTION IV is a system which employs this approach. It will be used here as a model for explaining how it functions. Figure 5 is a more expanded representation of the modules and their interrelationship than is shown in Fig. 3.

The process begins by accepting orders (requirements) for items to be manufactured. Such orders can be at any level of any product which exists on the bill-of-material file. Orders for items normally held in inventory are first processed by the Material Ordering Module, where they are netted against on-hand and on-order quantities and put into economic lot sizes. The Material Ordering Module uses the lot-size technique deemed most appropriate (by material planners) for each individual item.

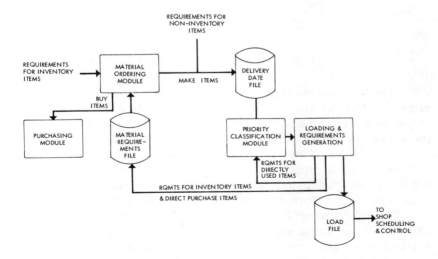

Figure 5. Integrated capacity and material requirements planning.

The resulting combined orders are merged with the orders for noninventory items and placed in a delivery date file which is sequenced according to requirement week. Orders required in later time periods are loaded by the system before those required in earlier time periods.

As each time period is encountered, all orders due in that time period are put into four priority classifications according to value of the item (whether piece part, subassembly, or final assembly). Items with the highest value are backward loaded first so that when orders are loaded to capacity limitations, the overall production plan will be one which tends to minimize work-in-process and inventory holding costs. This happens because jobs loaded later are more likely to encounter overload conditions and thus have to be "smoothed" to an earlier time period. All operations for an item are loaded before loading of the next item is begun.

Operation and set-up times for each operation are added to its designated work center. If an overload situation is encountered, the system first checks for a fit in alternative work centers previously defined by production planners. If overload conditions are encountered in all candidate work centers, the job is moved to the next earlier time period and the process is repeated.

Figure 6. Calculation of slack times between operations.

When sufficient capacity is found, the job is loaded and the elapsed times for the operation and set-up are calculated. Figure 6 graphically depicts how the slack time back to the operation that should precede the loaded operation is determined.

The "Pickup Time" is a parameter established by manufacturing engineers which represents the time needed to gather all the materials, piece parts, and tools required to perform the operation. Pickup time, therefore, is dependent on the item being processed.

The "Receiving Time" is based on problems encountered at a work center in being able to process a job once it arrives. It includes what most people refer to as queue time. Receiving time, therefore, is dependent on the work center in which the job is to be performed.

The "Transient Time" is the time it takes to move work from the work center where the preceding operation is performed to the next work center on the routing. PRODUCTION IV utilizes a transport matrix which contains move times between any two work centers in the system. Transit time, therefore, is dependent upon the relative locations of work centers.

The "Sending Time" is a parameter which accounts for time spent from completion of the preceding operation to transportation pickup. It includes inspection (if this is not a separate operation) and waiting for transportation. Send time, therefore, is dependent upon the work center where the preceding operation is to be performed.

The "Smoothing" is the amount of time the job has to be shifted backward in time because of overload conditions.

It is clear from this discussion that the integrated approach described here does not utilize standard lead times—in fact, it calculates lead times for each item that it loads. Two orders for the same item which have different due dates will most likely have different lead times. The calculated lead times are generated based on the relationship between planned load and planned capacity in the future. Standard lead times used in MRP are often based on management intuition based on past experience. This may have been adequate in the past when most manufacturing companies were able to get by with unbalanced inventories, longer lead times, and marginally efficient operations. Now competitive pressures, particularly from companies that are utilizing computers effectively, are forcing U.S. manufacturers to run their businesses with closer tolerances.

Once an operation is successfully loaded, a check is made to determine if that operation requires any material or parts. When the loaded operation requires a directly made component, the same lead time calculations described above are performed to determine the due date for the component. This component is then put into its priority classification for the time period in which it is due. It then awaits its turn for loading.

Should the loaded operation require an inventory article, a requirement for that article is put into a material requirements file combined with all other requirements for the same article, and is transmitted to the Material Ordering Module, where it is netted against on-hand and on-order quantities and combined into economic lot sizes. If the inventory article is a manufactured item, the requirement for the lot is placed in the delivery date file for loading. If the inventory article is a purchased item, the Purchasing Module generates a Purchase Order Suggestion when the requirement falls within the purchase lead time.

Order confirmation (upper right)

PHONE: TR 9540
TELEX: COPENHAGEN 22-112
ADDRESS: BOX 185 COPENHAGEN

ORDER NO. 712 022
DATE: 14 OCTOBER 1968
HANDLER:
OUR REF.: BJ
YOUR REF.:
TERMS OF PAYMENT: 21 DAYS NET

SANDBERG
HOVEDGADEN
AARHUS

OUR ART NO.	QUANT	QUANT UNIT	NAME AND QUALITY	UNIT PRICE KR	DELIVERY TIME YEAR	WEEK
22918120	350	PC	SKF-ROLLER BEARING NO. 291818	3.940	72	17
	150	PC			72	18
	250	PC			72	19
	250	PC			72	20
	350	PC			72	21
	250	PC			72	22
TOTAL	2000	PC		7,880.		

WE AWAIT ORDER CONFIRMATION

ALT SUPPLIERS

SUPPLIER	SUPPLIER NO. (TURNOVER TAX NO.)
BANG	1234560
TRESKMAN	2345670
OTRA	4567890
SANDBERG	5678900

STOCK

IN STOCK QUANT	CONSUMP THIS YR	QUANT UNIT	CONSUMP LAST YR.	STK LOC	SP. P., INV.	ANNUAL VOL	TERMS OF PAYMENT	MIN STK	OBSCL. WK. &CD.	FORECAST UNRES. CONS.	LAST ORDER WEEK	LAST WITH-DRAWAL WK	LAST INV COUNT. WK	TOTAL NO. OF ORDERS	LATE ORDERS %	AVER. LATE-NESS	LAST STND PR.CH.WK.	CONTROL CODE
2500.0	4705	PCS.	10521	D21	121.0	39921	21-NET			10.0	710	712	701	24	25%	1.5	552	1
							14-NET				705			51	10%	2.4		
							21-2.0				707			102	12%	0.2		
							14-2.0				650			10	30%	2.0		

PURCHASE

MIN ORD QUANT	PARTIAL DELIV ALLOW	MAX. ORD TM.HOR	DEL FREQ	WEIGHT PURCH. U	REJECT PCT	AVR. PURCH.U	SAFETY TIME	AVER. LATENESS	LEAD TIME	STANDARD PRICE	ST. PRICE INDEX	PACKAGE SIZE	CONVERSION FACTOR	UNIT PRICE	PURCHASE UNIT	SHORTAGE CODE	DEPLET WEEK	CUSTOMS NO.	BUYING GROUP
2000		20		0.10		350	0.5	1.8	06	3.50 .0	101	50		3.940		2	718 1		

SUGGESTED PURCHASE

ARTICLE NO.	QUANT.	Q. UNIT	UNIT PRICE	DELIVERY	LOTS
72291818120	2000	PCS.	3.940	717-722	6

SKF-ROLLER BEARING NO. 291818   B291818

FORMER ORDERS

SUPL.	SPL. NO	TERMS PAYM!	ORD.NO./ BID INV.	ORDERED/ RECEIVED	QUANT UNIT	WEEK (F & L)	UNIT PRICE	LAST ACT. THS
1	TRESKMAN	14-NET	620122	3000	PC	625		3.910
2	2345670	14-NET	630567	3000	PC	634	634	DEPLETION WK
	5678900	14-2.0		2590	PC	636		3.900 DEPLETION WK
3	5678900	14-2.0	639100	2400	PC	641	642	DEPLETION WK
	5678900	14-2.0		2000	PC	642		3.900 DEPLETION WK
4	1234560	21-NET	650002	1800	PC	648	650	DEPLETION WK
				2000	PC	701		3.940 DEPLETION WK
				2000	PC	710		

JOB	QUANT	JOB	QUANT	JOB	QUANT	JOB	QUANT
1234	200	2345	200	2346	20	7890	
4567	200	5678	50	6789			
8901	30						
1234	400						
2345	500			10			
3456	500	6789	10				
4567	600						
5678	500						
7890	600						

RESERVATIONS

WEEK	JOB	QUANT	JOB	QUANT	JOB	QUANT	JOB	QUANT
712	1234	200	2345	200	2346	200	7890	
713	4567	200	5678	50	6789	10		
714	8901	30						
715	1234	400						
716	2345	500						
717	3456	500	6789	10				
718	4567	600						
719	5678	500						
720	7890	600						

Figure 7. Order suggestion form.

Figure 7 is an example of an order suggestion provided by PRODUCTION IV. As can be seen, the order suggestion is made up of two parts. The right-hand side is an actual completed order form which can be detached and mailed to the vendor if it meets the approval of the Purchasing Department. The left-hand side contains a wealth of analytical data which can be used by the Material Controller and Purchasing Agent in making a decision on the suggestion. As illustrated, this data includes delivery performance of alternative vendors, stock status and statistics, purchase policies, recent orders, and gross requirements by time period.

Follow-up of order suggestions is provided by the system to assure that an order is placed and that it is confirmed by the supplier; in addition, reminders to suppliers are produced a short time before delivery, and overdue deliveries and delivery errors are reported.

Loading proceeds in this integrated approach down each structure path until started operations are encountered (as determined from floor reports) or purchased, or stocked components are encountered. One of the chief outputs from this intermediate level of planning and control is a load file. This is a file of all operations loaded into work centers and the time period in which each operation is loaded. The first few weeks of this file is the data that is used to drive the Shop Scheduling and Control Module. This latter module is a short-range planning tool.

Summary

In this paper, certain computerized tools that are becoming more readily available to manufacturers have been outlined. A comparison was made between tools that are integrated and those that are not. Certain advantages accrue to manufacturers that employ the integrated approach. However, it is newer on the American scene—although it has been used successfully in Europe since 1963—and the choice that a given manufacturer makes may depend on his management style.

At any rate, both approaches are in their infancy, and while startling successes will continue to occur, there will be enough failures to discourage the weak of heart.

Building Systems: "Canned" versus "Home-Brewed"

Robert A. Bonsack

Arthur Andersen & Co.
Santa Ana, California

Evaluating Production Control Software Packages

Buying and using computer software packages can be an effective method of stretching your data processing dollars. It can also lead to "systems suicide." The difference primarily depends on the approach used to select a software package. This discussion will outline a systematic approach for the identification, evaluation, and selection of software packages.

Why would "packages" be considered instead of a complete custom-designed software system? The answer lies in cost reductions, installation time reductions, improvements in operating effectiveness, and the ability to complement the in-house analyst experience.

Selecting and developing production control software has proven to be a particularly difficult area in which to generalize, because of the widely divergent and relatively complex design requirements. Here "production control" refers to the system for directing the orderly movement of goods through the entire manufacturing cycle, from the determination of production requirements and requisitioning of raw materials to the delivery of the finished product, and the system objectives are to improve customer service, minimize inventory investment, and maximize manufacturing efficiency.

In spite of the inherent difficulties, new computer hardware, when coupled with integrated data management-oriented systems software to handle the complex data interrelationships which exist in most manufacturing systems, provides the potential for improved production control systems. As might be expected, the cost and time required to design and install these highly computerized and vastly improved production control systems is very substantial. In response, new and improved design and installation aids and software packages have been developed to solve the cost-time problem. Many of these packages and approaches are comparatively new. Some have been poorly conceived and others carry the stigma which is frequently attached to "generalized" approaches. For these reasons and many others, manufacturing companies have generally been slow to accept them.

Types of Packages and Approaches

One common reason for the reluctance to use design aids and software packages is that the myriad of packages and approaches make the identification, evaluation, and selection process difficult. To better understand the scope and range of the available computer system aids, they can be categorized by broad type and characteristic as Application Software, Systems Software, and Systems Design and Installation Aids.

Application Software

The highest level, or most complete, would be application software. Application software packages vary greatly in the degree in which system and programming requirements for an application area are defined and coded. It is typical for company management to consider the installation of an application software package as being an essentially "turn-key" operation, i.e., plug it in and let it go. A brief review of the nature of most application packages is usually sufficient to bury this fallacy.

The phrase "off-the-shelf package" is probably most accurately applied to those fully coded, generalized programs which have been developed for service bureau-type use. Generally, these packages must be approached with the view that, where modifications are required, they will be reflected in changes to the internal operating procedures of the user company in order to accommodate the package design features.

IBM's PICS Requirements Planning application package is a good example of the type of application package which is fully coded, but as a part of the package design features, provides for user customized design features to meet optional design requirements.

Partially coded application packages which must be customized by extensive user logic are typical of packages which have been developed for those application areas which are extremely difficult to generalize. An example of this type of package is the IBM PICS Shop Floor Control package.

Systems Software

Systems software is a less comprehensive category than application software. Systems software would generally be used as the basis for a customer-developed package. Ideally, a company would like to find "the application systems package" which meets their design requirements and can be installed quickly with little or no modification. Unfortunately, all too often a company finds that no form of application package meets their design criteria. This means that the company must undertake the definition of a data base, file interrelationships, and the necessary input/output software to provide a foundation for their application processing. Since the systems software required to handle the functions of data management necessary in third-generation production control systems is extremely complex, it is a rare user who attempts to custom-develop his own systems software.

The first type of systems software frequently encountered is the data base management package such as IBM's original BOMP/DBOMP, CFMS, and Cincom's TOTAL. These systems software packages handle the data management for a set of logically interrelated files. The newer data base managers are capable of handling the complex network structures that more compactly and accurately depict the nature of a manufacturing company's data base.

Another type of systems software that is becoming increasingly popular is the packages which provide for data definition and standardized, packaged input validation and report generation. Representative of these packages are Informatic's MARK IV and Arthur Andersen & Co.'s LEXICON. Through the use of program modules which tailor the processing based on the characteristics of the data base, these packages are capable of performing most, if not all, of the programming normally required to validate input data and extract and format report records.

Due in part to the success attributable to the first two types of systems software mentioned, and also because of the need for more sophisticated systems software, a new type of more comprehensive systems software has begun to appear. These comprehensive data management systems, such as Burrough's Disk Forte and IBM's IMS-2, offer the features of the data base management packages plus other powerful data management functions. Features which may be found in these data management systems are teleprocessing communication control programs, comprehensive system security features such as file and data protection from unauthorized access, comprehensive backup/restart recovery functions, and internal "short-form" programming languages. However, the practical use of many of these systems would normally require a relatively sophisticated systems environment and large-scale computer hardware.

Since these data management systems provide only a technical foundation on which improved systems can be constructed, the need exists for the integration of the user's design features with the data management system in order to produce effective production control systems.

Systems Design and Installation Aids

For the purposes of this discussion, the most fundamental or basic level of software would be systems design and installation aids. Brochures and application manuals, e.g., IBM's PICS (Production Information and Control System) Application manual, and Honeywell's FACTOR (Integrated Factory Management System) manuals, which are associated with an application software package, are all useful aids.

Arthur Andersen & Co. has developed a comprehensive set of design aids called MAC-PAC (Arthur Andersen's manufacturing planning and control system). These detailed manuals contain representative manufacturing system design specifications and include discussions regarding the pros and cons of various production control strategies; for example, requirements planning versus reorder point. Included are input/output information matrices, system flow charts, and summarized program synopses.

MAC-PAC and several textbooks, such as *Production and Inventory Control Principles and Techniques* by Plossl and Wight, and a fairly recent video tape course could assist in design selection. This type of design aid is especially useful during the preliminary design for defining and selecting appropriate design features.

A new breed of design aids is the system design test packages which assist in the design selection by simulating performance of system alternatives. For example, Arthur Andersen & Co.'s STOCKIT is a system design test package capable of evaluating the design of inventory control systems by determining effective alternative ordering rules and service levels as a basis for reducing the inventory investment and ordering costs and improving customer service. IBM's IMPACT and Andersen's FORTEST are packages which can be used to evaluate and determine the effectiveness of alternative forecasting techniques. The use of quantitative system design test packages can significantly increase the effectiveness and reliability in selection of system design features.

Package Evaluation Techniques

The basic steps in selecting and evaluating software are as follows:

- develop system design requirements;
- develop selection criteria;
- prepare specifications questionnaire;
- assemble data and evaluate;
- negotiate contract.

Packages Are No Substitute for Systems Design

First and foremost in the evaluation process is the clear definition of the system's objectives and requirements. Since it is typical for software vendor literature to portray a package as an answer to every manufacturer's problems, it is essential to determine how the user company's specific production control objectives and operating problems fit into the framework of the "Utopian" solution. It is imperative that these production control characteristics and objectives be carefully defined before an attempt is made to establish the required system features, since the defined system features must be related to the characteristics and objectives. For example, a thorough job of identifying demand characteristics provides the basis for deciding whether reorder point planning, requirements planning, or a combination of both is required.

Having defined the business objectives, the next step is to proceed to a definition of required production control system design features. The system features and source and output information should be defined with and approved by production control management. Up to this point, the work required to evaluate and select a software package parallels those activities normally associated with the development of a customized system.

Establish Package Selection Criteria

Having defined the design features of the system, the user is in a position to establish the criteria for the selection of the package or design aids. The following selection criteria provide a base from which a company can develop its own criteria that meet the characteristics of its specific situation:

Package Design Feature Applicability Is the Primary Considera-tion. The most obvious (and important) consideration is the evaluation of how the design features of the package accommodate the required system design features identified in the preliminary systems design phase. Needless to say, unless a substantial portion of the design requirements is satisfied, it is doubtful that any further evaluation effort would be warranted. Since it is extremely probable that no package will completely satisfy all the design requirements, an evaluation must be made to establish the relative ease and flexibility necessary to modify and customize the package to satisfy the user's unique requirements.

One company that manufactures a fairly complex product was experiencing considerable difficulty in planning material requirements because rapid sales growth had made their manual explosion procedure too cumbersome and unreliable. Requirements planning was being done weekly with a planning horizon of approximately 6 months. They quickly searched for a package to solve their problem and chose one based upon the low sales price and the fast installation time quoted by the salesmen. After the contract had been signed and the system had been run for several weeks, they found the system had a planning horizon of only eight periods—or 8 weeks in their case. This was totally unsatisfactory for planning any of their purchase part requirements. Because of the dynamic nature of their business, monthly planning periods were, unfortunately, not a satisfactory solution. Modifications to the package were required and neither the low cost nor fast installation time originally planned was achieved. This planning horizon is one of the key features which should have been specified when selecting a requirement planning package.

The Quality of Package Documentation Directly Affects Implementation Cost and Success. The quality of documentation provided by the package vendor will be apparent by the ease of the review and evaluation of the package design features. Examples of the type of documentation required to review the package design features are sample formatted output reports, an inventory of the detail data file specifications and required data elements, system flow charts, and system control features such as run-to-run controls and the batch balancing of input transactions. If modifications to the package are likely, a careful review of the program documentation should be made. This documentation should include block diagrams supported by a program narrative and program listings. Poor detailed documentation will mean the customization effort will be prolonged and more costly. Since the coded programs are but one segment of the effort required in the design and installation of a system, the absence or presence of documentation, such as clerical procedures, key-punch instructions, and computer operating instructions to aid in the installation and conversion, must be ascertained. Where documentation is weak, it is likely that modification and installation of the system will be far more costly than if the package were adequately documented.

The next common pitfall is analogous to the problem the typical father has on Christmas Eve when he attempts to put unassembled children's toys together. In the showroom window, the assembled toy was a model of operating efficiency, but attempting to assemble it from the grossly inadequate instructions is a herculean task. Similarly, a software package may be a paragon of operating efficiency in benchmarks and other demonstrations, but the lack of supporting documentation may significantly impede the installation of the package in a user company.

In some cases we have found that technically sound computer systems have failed because user personnel were not provided with sufficient documentation to understand system processing or responsibilities in terms of system input. In the last year and a half, software companies have cut their package installation prices to the bare minimum to encourage sales. In many cases, training of client personnel has been all but eliminated in their installation estimates. Without very complete documentation, these systems fail because user personnel cannot operate the systems. The situation is particularly prevalent where the package is leased from a rather small software firm with limited resources. Their entire existence depends on their maintaining control over the computer programs, and they are reluctant to supply detailed system logic. They fear someone will copy the programs and drive them out of business.

The Ease of Package Interface with Existing and Planned Application Systems Should Be Carefully Evaluated. The ease of interfacing the package with existing and planned application systems will be a significant factor in the success and acceptability of the installed system. Unless the input, output, and operating interface between the package and installed or planned application systems are reasonably compatible, it is likely that costly and impractical modifications will be necessary. Packages can usually be best employed where interface requirements are minimal.

In one case, a factory payroll package had to be modified to feed labor distribution information into the company's mechanized accounting system. The cost of these modifications almost equaled the purchase price of the payroll package.

Operating Effectiveness and Cost Can Be Significant Factors.
The vendor should provide the potential user with processing timing
estimates based on user volumes and factored by system parameters
and processing options from which some rough estimates of the
execution time can be made. Later in the evaluation process, when
the field of potential packages has been reduced, it will be highly
desirable for the user to use "benchmark" programs to permit a
detailed evaluation of actual package performance. Reviewing the
system flow chart, run-to-run documentation, and operating instructions will provide a fairly reliable basis for judging the ease of
operating the system. This can be substantiated when actual benchmarks are performed. Excessive set-ups and operator intervention
will detract from the acceptability of the package.

It is in this area that many software packages have failed. In
companies that have a large number of parts and bills of material, the
processing time can destroy the usefulness of the system. IBM's
requirements planning system is ideal for limited data volumes, but
when applied to companies with large part and bill of material
volumes the system is very difficult to implement successfully. Computer processing time at one company approached 50 hours per
planning cycle. This limited planning to a monthly basis and required
a staff of roughly 20 men to adjust requirements during the month.
Processing time can be reduced at some companies by using the "net
change" feature in Requirements Planning, but it may not solve the
problem if there are significant master schedule, engineering, or
inventory balance changes. Changes to the data base must be included in "Net Change" processing, or the results will be inaccurate.
Including these changes in "Net Change" processing can significantly
increase the computer processing time. Many large companies found
they cannot successfully implement weekly material requirements
using packaged products because of processing time limitations.

IBM has now recognized this problem and has inserted instructions in their manuals on how an estimate of the computer
processing time can be calculated prior to system installation. If
timing estimates are made during the package evaluation period the
user should be able to evaluate the applicability of the software.

*Data Processing Equipment and Computer Software Necessary
To Support the Package Are Key Selection Factors.* In the economic
evaluation of the software packages, not only must the nucleus price
of the package be considered, but it is also imperative that "add-on"
costs in terms of equipment and supporting software be a direct
factor in the evaluation. Vendor literature should provide sufficient
information from which the core storage required to operate the

system can be accurately calculated. For example, a user desiring to use a comprehensive data management system may be forced to upgrade his equipment and would be faced with a costly operating system conversion or service bureau charges. Even a cursory review can be of substantial assistance in narrowing the list of candidates; e.g., if a software package requires 100K of core and the user has a 32K machine, that package may be eliminated from consideration.

Care should be taken when selecting software, if there is some possibility that a future change in computer hardware suppliers may be possible. In many cases, particularly where file organization software is used, the system is virtually locked into that brand of hardware. It is only natural that equipment salesmen push the implementation of these packages, many of which are free, to insure that they will not lose the account. Packages which are built using a simple sequentially organized data base and programmed in COBOL can be run on a variety of machines with little conversion cost. This can be important in the selection of the software package.

Analysis of Vendor Reputation and Services Is Desirable. An analysis of vendor reputation and services, and reference to other package users, is a desirable preliminary screening criterion. The stability and financial position of the vendor should be investigated. This will provide some indication of quantity and quality of implementation assistance and field support which can reasonably be expected from vendor personnel. A bankrupt vendor will be of little or no assistance. Certainly some element of financial soundness is required for the vendor to maintain a technical support team for the package.

The user should request the vendor to provide a list which identifies specific customers, if any, who are using the package, indicating the customer's type of industry, the date on which the package was implemented and the period of package use. Having identified customers, the user should follow up by selectively contacting users to determine their satisfaction with the software, documentation, and support. Other users often provide insight into detailed technical idiosyncracies and problems which can only be gained through actually working with the package. Or, you can be a pioneer hero and be the first "satisfied user," or perhaps a "victim."

It is important here that the investigation of references go beyond the data processing manager. User personnel outside of the data processing area should be contacted with regard to the operation of the package. Many systems which are deemed successful to data processing personnel are viewed somewhat differently by user personnel.

One company bought a package which had been installed at several other companies with success. This company wanted only a portion of the package and later found, in spite of promises, that the system would not run without all segments installed.

Recurring Software Costs and Contract Terms May Vary Significantly between Vendors. Where the vendor offers the package for either purchase or lease, it will be necessary to perform a lease-buy analysis. The expected life of the system is an important factor in this analysis. The user must also consider the possibility that the level of vendor support for purchased software may be less than if the package were leased. Particularly, where there are a fairly large number of users, it might be expected that lease users will be assigned a higher priority than purchase users where competition exists for support resources. We have certainly seen this in the performance of certain hardware manufacturers in their favored maintenance of rental equipment versus purchased equipment.

It is also important, before any long-term lease or purchase is negotiated, that a clear need for the system exist. In one actual case, the system's problems were solved by the addition of two clerical personnel. Unfortunately, a contract for a mechanized system had been signed which cost $15,000 per month including computer processing time. The output of this system was not as good as that provided by the two additional clerks, and the mechanical system was not used. The company was forced to pay the $15,000 per month contract price over the term of the lease agreement.

Degree of Reduction in Design and Installation Cost and Project Duration Is a Key Summary Evaluation Factor. Using the cost and time required to custom-design and install "the production control system" as a base, and relating the preceding criteria to the required design and installation tasks, the user should be able to estimate the cost-time savings he reasonably expects to gain through the selection of a package.

Source reporting procedures, data validation, and file maintenance programs required to support the data base used by a package are often not properly evaluated. Thus, the implementation effort tends to be grossly underestimated. One company recently installed a requirements planning system. Of the total 48 man-months of the systems and programming time expended on this project, only 6 percent (or 3 man-months) of the time was required to customize the vendor software. The remaining 94 percent of the time was required to design and implement the supporting data maintenance programs and user source reporting procedures.

After the user has established the selection criteria, he should assign weights to each of the criteria. By using a system of weighted criteria, when the identification and evaluation steps have been carefully completed, the objective selection of the required package can be largely quantified.

Systematic Approach to Evaluating and Selecting Software

Up to this point, the user has established the criteria and established an objective format for the identification of the best package solution. The following suggested approach for package evaluation and selection relies on this previous work in order to identify quickly and accurately the appropriate software package.

Preliminary Screening. Rather than becoming immersed in the detail of a host of packaged solutions, the user can do some quick preliminary screening to narrow the field. There are a number of reference sources that provide information regarding available software packages, such as ICP QUARTERLY, DATA PRO 70, and AUERBACH SOFTWARE REPORTS.

Hardware salesmen are an obvious source of data on manufacturers' packages. Since consulting firms have not generally listed their packages in these references, it would be appropriate to arrange to meet with consultants to discuss the scope of their services and the availability of packages—their own, if any, as well as other sources.

When this initial review of candidates is completed, it would be unusual to expect more than three or four packages which indicate that they merit more detailed review and analysis.

Detailed Analysis and Evaluation. Drawing upon the resources and documentation obtained as a result of doing the preliminary design, a uniform software package specification questionnaire should be prepared for distribution to all the remaining vendor candidates.

The depth and degree to which the questionnaire is utilized should be based on the relative cost and risks of the subject packages. Typically, the questionnaire will include much of the material identified in the process of preliminary design, e.g., output records, required system design features, etc.

The use of a questionnaire has several distinct advantages. It forces the vendor's response to be oriented toward the package's applicability to the user's unique production control design requirements rather than simply being a monologue of package features. Perhaps the most significant point is that it provides a consistent format for comparison of vendor responses and makes review and evaluation easier and more accurate.

The review and analysis of the vendors' responses to the questionnaire should be systematically evaluated using the weighted package selection criteria that have been previously developed. This will result in an objective analysis of the package design features.

After the vendor specifications have been evaluated, it is desirable to conduct actual benchmarks of the remaining packages, preferably on the user's own equipment. This will verify that the package is actually complete and operating and provide a basis for substantiating vendor claims as to core requirements and the operating effectiveness of the system. This is the last point at which deficiencies can be identified.

An analysis of package economics is particularly necessary where a choice must be made between competing vendors' packages or where there must be a decision made as to whether the system should be custom-designed or a package utilized, i.e., "a make-buy" analysis. For this reason, the cost and duration required to design and install a custom system should be used as the base point.

By relating the package features, documentation, and other installation aids to the full spectrum of activities required in the detail design and installation of a production control system, the tangible one-time implementation costs and projected net operating costs or savings should be quantifiable for each activity. Aside from tangible, readily quantifiable, economic considerations, there should be other measurable, intangible benefits that will prove difficult, if not impossible, to quantify. Illustrative of these types of intangible benefits are the improved effectiveness of management and improved customer service levels.

The results of the economic evaluation, coupled with the evaluation of package features and operating effectiveness, provide a sound basis upon which the project team can confidently base their conclusions.

Contract Negotiation: Select the Best Alternative

Having systematically performed the preceding activities, the choice of a package may be clear. However, it is possible that conflicting results of the package design feature evaluation and economic analysis may force further consideration. Consequently, the negotiation of contract terms may prove to be the determining factor in the decision process. Some of the contract points which should be considered are:

· provision for maintenance and training support;

· documentation and updating procedures;

· penalties for late performance or nonperformance;

- provision for free equipment;

- multi-installation use;

- contract renewal terms;

- price and credit terms.

The user's contract objectives should be thoroughly reviewed with his attorney so that the final contract provisions meet the user's contract objectives. Failure to carefully negotiate contract terms pertaining to monthly software rental or outside processing charges and charges to modify the package could result in costs which greatly exceed the original estimate. This is the one item that may, as a final resort, insure that the vendor fulfills the expectations promised in the specification book.

Summary

In summary, the following points have particular significance in the selection of software packages and design and installation aids for reducing implementation cost and duration, and for increasing the operating effectiveness of production control systems. Special emphasis should be placed on how the design features of the package relate to the design features the user has developed to meet the business characteristics and operating objectives. Remember that a package is no substitute for the system design effort required of the user.

An attempt to shortcut or reduce the required systematic steps which must be performed to select an appropriate package will result in an incomplete evaluation of software packages which may be misleading and costly. The user should insist on reviewing all package documentation, meeting with personnel in other companies that have installed the package to discuss their experience, and running bench-marks to aid in negotiating a clear and satisfactory contract. Since it would be unusual to expect a "Washington's Birthday Sale" on a software package, the user should resist vendor pressure to make a hurried commitment to a software package until he has systematically completed all the steps in the evaluation.

Particular attention should be paid to the tendency of users to understate the systems and programming effort not directly related to the package itself, but necessary to make the package an effective operating system. The estimate of software package savings must relate to the entire spectrum of activities required to design and install a system.

The learning curve in working with software packages is steep. Where possible, attempt to utilize personnel with prior experience and the competency to work effectively with software packages. By following the systematic step-by-step approach outlined, it is possible to select software packages that will significantly reduce the cost and duration of the design and implementation of production control systems. The one-time implementation cost required for a comprehensive custom system might be reduced by as much as 40 percent; 16 percent by design and installation aids, 20 percent by systems software and 4 percent by application software.

The user, through the correct approach to identification, evaluation, and selection of software, can translate this package potential into less costly and more timely and effective production control systems.

Managing Systems Development Projects

L. J. Burlingame

Vice President, Materials Management
Twin Disc, Incorporated
Racine, Wisconsin

In his movie on implementing a Material Requirements Planning system ("MRP Outputs and How to Use Them"), Mr. Walter Goddard, Executive Vice President of Oliver Wight, Inc., used the following seven divisions of manufacturing systems development. They are:

1. management commitment

2. program specifications

3. programming and debugging

4. procedure documentation

5. user training

6. conversion planning

7. operation mode

I believe that these divisions are a useful way in which to look at the problems of systems development and management. I further believe that the movie itself, which can be obtained through IBM or through the National Office of the American Production and Inventory Control Society, is a very worthwhile effort.

I will discuss each of these areas in some detail. However, Fig. 1 exhibits my own interpretation of these seven areas as they appear, to me, more meaningfully. You will note that I have changed a few of the names and I have tried to show them on a time scale with the appropriate overlaps which indicate that they are not in any way separate from each other. The layout of Fig. 1 suggests a network of events similar to those used by PERT or CPM. I think the analogy to these two more complex systems is appropriate, although I do not feel that it is necessary for the average project to actually operate one of these systems. There is a need, however, to try to be thorough

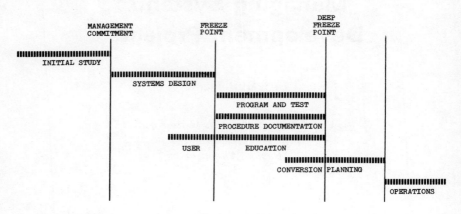

Figure 1.

in your planning, and the creation of a network, whether it is used later or not, is extremely useful in forcing people to plan each and every event.

I have renamed Phase I from "Management Commitment" to "Initial Study." The Initial Study Phase is ended with a management commitment. It has often been said that it is necessary to be a small company in order to achieve beneficial results from a computer system, and I think this charge was substantially true, in the beginning. However, recently, there have been enough large companies making substantial, if not spectacular, progress that we must give up the idea that only a small company can be successful. I think it is useful to look at the differences between small and large companies in the past in order to see what lessons have been learned so that success can become more frequent. It is in the Initial Study and the next step, Systems Design, that most of the difference between the large company and a small one is to be noticed. Figure 2 is a flow chart of the Initial Study Phase of a project as we use it at Twin Disc. You will note that the exclusive responsibility for this Initial Study is borne by the using department. I think herein lies the apparent difference between large companies and small. The large companies, with their very adequate resources, have tended to assign the Initial Study Phase to Systems Engineers from the Data Processing Department. The smaller companies all wished they had the resources to do that but they settled for the second best that they could manage. In this case, second best turned out to be first best, and user involvement, if not user control, in the Initial Study Phase, is an accepted process today. Therefore, I think we accept the principle that if the

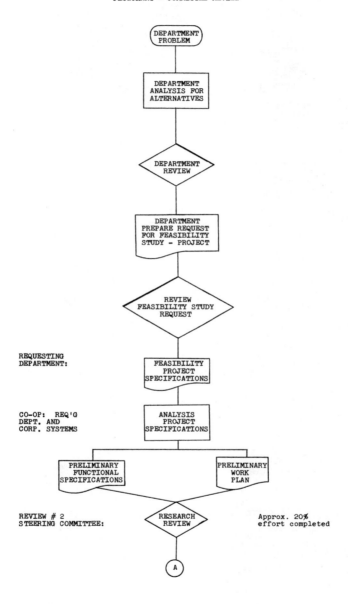

FLOWCHART - COMMITTEE REVIEW

Figure 2. (Continued on following page.)

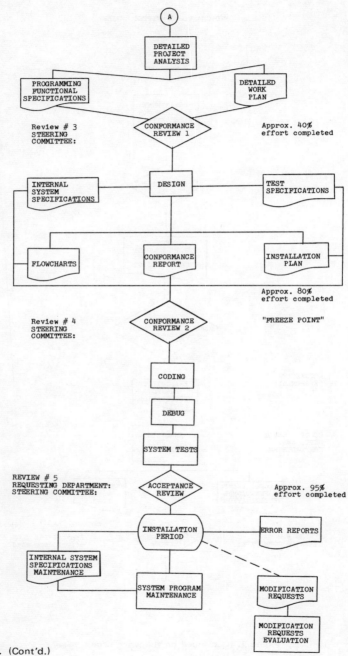

Figure 2. (Cont'd.)

using department is unwilling to supply talent of the highest caliber, the chances for success are minimal.

Figure 3 shows a writeup of the information required as input to our Data Processing Steering Committee prior to their considera- tion of a new product. I repeat, this input is exclusively the respon- sibility of the using department. Your attention is called to the paragraph on output requirements, which is typical of the detail required. It may seem that we are cutting it a little fine, but our insistence on user development of this kind of detail eliminates a great deal of misunderstanding later in the project. When a project has been submitted to the Steering Committee (which is chaired by the Executive Vice President) and accepted, a commitment from management has, in fact, been given.

At Twin Disc we have divided the Systems Design Phase into a preliminary and final phase, which are represented by Fig. 3. I think the important thing to note about this, and also about systems design in general, is that there are at nearly all times parallel activities by Data Processing and the user department. You will note, going back to Fig. 1, that I have skipped down to step No. 5 chronologically and suggest that User Education should begin prior to the end of Systems Design. There are two basic and very good reasons for this. One is that user education is perhaps the most important single step in assuring success, and it would be impossible to overemphasize it. The other is that you will get useful input to the Systems Design Phase from the User Education Phase. When implementing our critical ratio dispatching system at Twin Disc, we had sufficient input from our foremen's group during the User Education Phase that we made major changes in our total system. This was in spite of the fact that there were two foremen involved in the initial study task force.

I have suggested that the Systems Design Phase be ended with a freeze point. This freeze point is a little like the freeze point in an engineering design project, in that it means less that things are actually completely frozen than it means changes will be resisted. As a matter of fact, there is an excellent analogy between design engineering of a product and the design of a computer system. Almost across-the-board principles applied to one will prove bene- ficial when applied to the other.

Programming and Testing and Procedure Documentation are two steps where Data Processing becomes more active than the using department. Up until this time, the user has been required to put forth 80 to 90 percent of the effort. This probably turns around in this phase. However, we still see user involvement in the testing and writing of operating procedures. Our programming section makes use

STANDARD OPERATING PROCEDURES
TWIN DISC, INCORPORATED

ISSUED BY	APPROVAL:	EFFECTIVE DATE	STANDARD OPERATING PROCEDURE NO.
		July 1, 1968	11.020
CORP. SYSTEMS APPROVAL		REVISION NO.	PAGE
			12 OF 13

TITLE

Management Information Systems Steering Committee

EXHIBIT II
REQUEST FOR FEASIBILITY STUDY
CONTENTS

TITLE PAGE

Title, date, author.

TABLE OF CONTENTS

Sections, exhibits, appendices, page references.

ABSTRACT OF APPLICATION

Introduction, description of major objectives, scope, relationships to other systems, major users and uses of the system output, special problems, summary of costs and benefits.

OUTPUT REQUIREMENTS

Definition of final content of all reports, rough draft of report formats, description of use of each report, number of copies and distribution of reports.

INPUT REQUIREMENTS

Complete identification of input data required including an estimate of the daily and/or weekly and/or monthly and/or quarterly and/or yearly volume of records, the content of the records, master or continuously updated records required and their volume, various kinds of transaction records to be processed, and a description of each type of input record's use.

PROCESSING SUMMARY

Description of operations to be performed on the input records to produce the output reports. This must include mathematical formulas, special conditions which require special operations such as exceptions, restrictions and limitations for specific conditions which are known to exist with reasonable regularity.

CONTROL AND BALANCING

Definitions of input preparations which are or should be used to establish controls to insure that all input transaction records for the computer run have been processed. Also any criteria for the data contained in the input transaction record to check as proof of its validity.

ERROR CORRECTION

Procedures and criteria for error detection, correction and re-entry.

SCHEDULE

Timing requirements for input, processing, output.

GLOSSARY

Definition of any special user-oriented terminology.

Figure 3.

of a great many tools to monitor their own effectiveness in these two areas. However, in general, I think people do a rather good job of this, and it is the areas in which mistakes are made that later cause difficulties. I have ended the Programming and Testing Phase, the Procedure Documentation Phase, and the User Education Phase at the same point in time, which we might call the "Deep Freeze Point." Since user education never really ends, it is somewhat arbitrary to cut it off here.

The next event, "Conversion Planning," starts well before the programming and testing is finished and continues right up to operations. There are three generally discussed methods of conversion. The first of these is Dr. Joseph Orlicky's so-called "Cold Turkey Conversion." This has become modified by Mr. Goddard to be called the "Dead Turkey Conversion," and Mr. Goddard is probably correct. However, since I have made three major conversions in the manufacturing area in the cold turkey mode and have been scarred but not killed, I know from first-hand experience that it can work. Dr. Orlicky points out that if you have done the previous five steps well enough, there is no doubt about the success of your conversion and, therefore, no point in not going across the board. I believe this is valid if you grant the premise.

Another method is the so-called "Running Parallel" method, and I can almost say, categorically, that with manufacturing systems, this does not work. The reason for this is that the data begins to differ between your old system and your new system, and you don't know which one to follow. You probably wind up following the old one because you are more familiar with the old. Therefore, you never get your new one, no matter how good, up and running. The third method of conversion is the most generally accepted today. It is the "Pilot Method." This simply means that you take one plant (a small one) or perhaps even one production line or department that can be considered separate from the rest of the business, and try your system out on it. When you have been successful in a small area, you are now safe to extend the conversion to the rest of the operation. I have not identified the end point of this phase. Perhaps it should be called "Fire the Project Manager" if a successful conclusion is not in sight. Certainly, if the preceding phases have been handled correctly, there can be very little excuse for failure at this point.

The only significant thing to say about operations, I guess, is that, to some extent, all six of the previous phases must continue at a reduced pace. Just as we previously drew the analogy between the product and a computer system, in the design phase there is an analogy in operations. Product improvements are always possible and desirable, and in today's world, anybody with a completely frozen attitude or position will quickly find himself obsolete. In the early 1960s, we made quite a thorough study of a company which had, in our opinion, the finest production and inventory control system we had ever seen. We felt so strongly about this that our initial work in the material requirements planning area was, to some extent, patterned on this company. Less than 5 years later, they were actively studying our system in the hope that they could catch up. They had neglected their system for so long that it was not even going to be possible to modify it and update it. They were required to start all over from scratch. There is no reason that you have to be a pioneer or inventor, but there is every reason that you not be last.

Potential Improvements and How To Measure Them

George W. Plossl

President, G. W. Plossl & Co., Inc.
Decatur, Georgia

The theme of this Symposium, "Profit Opportunities and New Challenges for Computers," is most appropriate, since the greatest opportunity for improving profits today lies in improving manufacturing management control systems. There is literally nothing a management team can do today which has the potential for improving return on investment like improved control of inventories and production. My new book is entitled *Manufacturing Control: The Last Frontier for Profits* (Reston, Virginia: Reston Publishing Company, 1973) and I truly believe this. Profit improvement activities such as new product development, process developments, marketing programs or methods, and standards improvements are whittling techniques compared to improved control which can simultaneously slash costs and thus increase profits while it reduces the assets required to earn them. Only manufacturing control simultaneously affects both parts of this measurement ratio.

The computer is only beginning to prove itself in this field. There have been very few successes and many failures to date. In one of the News Notes which our firm publishes, I listed what I thought were the most important deterrents. Quoting from News Note #1:

Too Many Other Problems To Solve First

Sometimes it's "Too few orders," meaning time for belt tightening; no money for such programs. Or, more likely, now it's, "Too many orders," meaning too much fire-fighting; no time or people available. "Reorganization" is another good alibi; how can anything start until the right "professional" is aboard? Isn't it first necessary to realign critical departments? New products must be introduced and no resources will be available to work on anything else. All of these are good reasons to postpone action on Material Requirement Planning (MRP)—or are they?

Can't Get the Basic Data Straightened Out

While the on-hand and on-order balances are always tough, the real bugaboos are bills of material and missing part numbers, not yet assigned to raw materials, semifinished components, and manufactured subassemblies.

Can't Develop a Master Production Schedule

Finished product options and variations appear to make it impossible to tell the materials plan how many of what will be made when. Product differences are highly visible; similarities and common elements are obscure.

Can't Get Around Systems Specialists Formalities

Production and inventory control practitioners unfamiliar with the computer and the needed programs are overawed and helpless when systems staff groups have different priorities and rigid, formal procedures. Nothing gets started until all of the program has been specified in detail. Guaranteed to stop MRP every time.

Too Little Commitment

Management is not sold on the need for MRP by vague and suspect benefits. The users lack confidence in their ability to control their own destiny and are reluctant to "stick their necks out." Other departments such as marketing, engineering, and cost accounting see nothing in it for them and haven't time to dig in and find out if perhaps there is.

Too Much Thinking, Too Little Doing

It's safer to study alternatives, double-check suggestions, challenge decisions, require more proof. Thinkers and debaters outnumber the doers who would make some decisions and go.

All these deterrents vanish when the specific benefits from improving control of manufacturing operations are identified. It is obvious to me that the first step necessary for success is to identify the specific savings which could be realized, together with other intangible benefits in the three important areas of customer service, manufacturing expense, and inventory investment. In every company

- *FORECAST*
  Demand – Production

- *PLAN PRIORITIES*
  Degree of control
  What items
  How much
  When

- *PLAN CAPACITY*
  Target inventory levels
  How much
  When

- *CONTROL CAPACITY*
  Input / Output

- *CONTROL PRIORITIES*
  Select
  Schedule / Reschedule
  Load / Reload
  Dispatch
  Expedite

Figure 1. Elements of production and inventory control.

where this has been done there has been no difficulty in getting management to assign the necessary resources. The only way to insure continuity of effort over the fairly long periods of time required to complete such programs, during which most companies experience many other demands on management time and corporate resources and changes in top management personnel, is to identify significant potential savings. There is no substitute for this.

A major development in production control in the last few years was the identification of the elements necessary in the system required for effective control of inventories and production. Figure 1 shows these elements. The major subdivisions are Forecasting, Planning, and Controlling Priorities and Planning and Controlling Capacity. Before this structure was identified, production control was viewed as "a collection of loosely related techniques," and there was too little success in applying the techniques, primarily because there was no appreciation of the way they had to be worked together in a system.

All planning, of course, begins with a forecast. Two forecasts are needed—one of customer demand and one of production to be scheduled to meet this demand. The latter is usually called the Master Production Schedule and is the result of the activities of Production or Business Planning. Priority Planning begins with a classification of inventories to determine how best to use the (usually scarce) resources of men, time, and money. The most familiar technique is the A-B-C classification which identified the vital few ("A") items which comprise the bulk of the value of materials flowing through an operation as contrasted to the many trivial "C" items. Since resources are rarely adequate to do an equal job of controlling all items, it is obviously sound management to devote most attention to the vital few and use simplified, inexpensive techniques for reording the trivial many. The excess inventories which result in the "C" classifications are sound insurance against difficulties arising from shortages. The "B" items are given middle-of-the-road treatment. The balance of priority planning involves applying one of the two basic ordering systems (Order Point/Order Quantity or Material Requirements Planning) to determine what item should be ordered, when, and in what quantities.

Capacity Planning begins with a determination of desired changes in total inventory levels. If inventories are to be reduced, sales (shipments) must exceed production and vice versa. Capacity required, both in manpower and plant equipment, will therefore be more or less than is needed to meet customer demand, depending on whether inventories are to be increased or decreased. More detailed planning may be necessary to determine how much capacity will be needed (and when) in each of the significant centers.

Capacity control involves employing the techniques of measuring production input and output rates from the significant work centers and comparing these measurements to the planned rates. This element is probably the most vital in the whole system. It is really the only true control which management can exercise. If a company does not have capacity adequate to make enough product it will have no success in making the right items at the right time.

Control of priorities can be extremely complex. Wherever possible, particularly in starting or so-called "gateway" work centers, orders should be selected for release equal to the capacity of the work center to handle them. Inventory planning systems, however soundly designed, do not generate work at a level rate nor at a rate equal to the capacity of the plant. Some means must be introduced to override the ordering system and feed work to a plant to match its capacity. Only after this is done can scheduling and the other priority control activities be effective. Scheduling assigns dates to significant operations to provide milestones so that progress through the manufacturing operations can be tracked. Since most businesses are getting more dynamic, rescheduling is probably a more appropriate title for this activity.

After orders have been scheduled, it is possible to measure the load impact on specific work centers and even on individual machines. This is the ancient technique of Machine Loading which until very recently has been almost completely ineffective. Notice that its function is priority control, not capacity control. It is used to determine if the specific capacity of individual work centers will be adequate to handle work in the desired priority sequence. It directs management's attention to the need for short-term capacity changes such as overtime, subcontracting, and alternate operations.

Dispatching includes all the necessary details of getting work started. Machines and operators must be selected: blueprints, routing sheets, set-up instructions, and other paper work must be provided. The last element, Expediting, will, unfortunately, always be with us. It will never be possible to plan everything so precisely that some informal system of reacting to unexpected changes will be unnecessary.

It is easy to see how important the computer is in production planning and control. The system just described is really *an information system* dealing with facts, figures, dates, quantities, and other bits of information which are the stock in trade of computers. While many good things can be done manually on these system elements, most companies will require a computer to be fully effective. Computer programs are useful in all elements of the system.

The proper sequence of activities to be followed is shown in Fig. 2. This is organized in four quandrants, one for each of the major activities of planning and controlling priorities and capacity. The master production schedule is the driving force for all planning and control activities. Priority and capacity planning must be interlocked for both long- and short-range operations. As illustrated in Fig. 2, capacity planning requires two steps, a first cut made at the finished product level (using average labor and machine content, for example) and a more detailed analysis at the component level. The latter uses planned orders from the material planning system indicating how many of what component will be manufactured in what period of time. Priority and capacity control are also linked; the planned priorities cannot be followed unless adequate capacity is available in individual work centers in specific time periods.

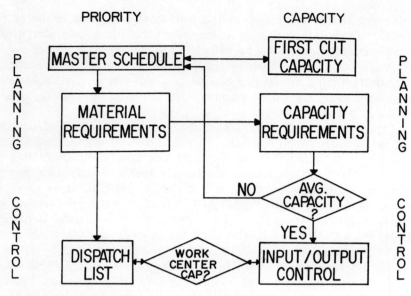

Figure 2. The sequence of activities in production planning and control.

As mentioned earlier, the potential benefits from improved manufacturing control exceed those of any other profit improvement activity. Figure 3 shows a checklist of items to consider in evaluating specific reductions in inventory investment and operating expense as well as improved customer service. The experience of companies successful in designing and installing manufacturing control systems has been to achieve significant benefits in all three areas. Each company may have items in addition to those listed in Fig. 3 which should be added to this list.

Even more important than these specific benefits are the intangible results of improved management under control. The ability to call promptly to management's attention a significant increase in demand, the need for a decrease in output, or undesirable changes in inventory levels can hardly be overvalued. The alternative to detecting change early and beginning corrective action promptly is reacting too late with inevitable over-correction and costly excesses. One company in heavy manufacturing customarily had backlogs increase sharply after their business picked up because of their inability to detect the increased demand and react quickly. It usually took them about a year to restore backlogs to normal levels. This meant long periods with dissatisfied customers. With an effective control system operating in 1972, they reacted promptly to the

BENEFITS

INVENTORY INVESTMENT
  STOCKED COMPONENTS
  SAFETY STOCK
  LOT SIZE REMNANTS
  OBSOLETE
  UNIQUE VS. COMMON
  FINISHED PRODUCT
  SERVICE PARTS

OPERATING EXPENSE
  SET-UP AND CHANGE-OVER
  UNPLANNED OVERTIME
  SUB-CONTRACT
  DOWNTIME
  INDIRECT LABOR
  PRODUCTIVITY
  WAREHOUSE, TAXES, INSURANCE

CUSTOMER SERVICE
  SALES
  FREIGHT
  SUBSTITUTES
  BACK-ORDERS
  CLERICAL, MAIL, TELEPHONE

PROMPT PLANNED RESPONSE

COORDINATED MANAGEMENT

Figure 3. Checklist of potential benefits in improved manufacturing control.

sharpest upturn in their career, restoring backlogs to suitable levels in approximately 3 months.

When sufficiently detailed and accurate information is available, a management team can pull together to solve the major problems of the business. Looking at management in many companies might easily convince you of the truth of Pogo's statement, "We have met the enemy and they are us." Marketing, manufacturing, engineering, and other departments are more frequently fighting among themselves than against competition. In the first 3 months of 1973, however, I was privileged to sit in top-level meetings in three companies in which the management teams were wrestling with a serious problem. In each case, capacity was inadequate to meet total demand. These teams, instead of pointing accusing fingers at each other, were concentrating their efforts on deciding which customers would receive product and which would not, which product line profit margins did not justify using the scarce capacity to manufacture them and what alternative courses were available to increase capacity quickly and economically. The benefits of this kind of coordinated management are obvious.

My basic purpose is to discuss the specific measurements used to determine whether or not benefits are being achieved. Such measures should be set up at the beginning of any program for systems development. Together with evaluating the benefits, this is a necessary first step to insure that proper priority is assigned to the effort, to get commitment from management, and to set benchmarks for checking future progress in achieving the goals. Estimates should be conservative; it is not necessary to develop "blue sky" numbers. I have yet to see a company fail to identify benefits large enough to justify the effort necessary to achieve them. Measures should be simple and easily understood. It is better to use other people's numbers wherever possible, rather than setting up new and untested indices. Use the measures of customer service Marketing now has. Take existing productivity figures from older reports familiar to management. Use turnover ratios developed in the past. Measures regularly produced by departments other than those engaged in

MEASURES

INVENTORY LEVELS
>TURNOVER
>INVENTORY/SALES RATIOS
>WEEKS WORK-IN-PROGRESS
>INVENTORY INPUT-OUTPUT:
>>PURCHASES VS. PLAN
>>LABOR VS. BUDGET
>>SHIPMENTS (ORDERS) VS. FORECAST
>>INVENTORY VS. BUDGET
>UNSHIPPED BACKLOG

CUSTOMER SERVICE
>PERCENT ITEMS IN STOCK:
>>FINISHED GOODS
>>COMPONENTS
>>SPARE PARTS
>PERCENT ORDERS BACKORDERED
>PERCENT PRODUCED ON TIME, "X" WEEKS LATE
>PRODUCTION VS. MASTER SCHEDULE

OPERATIONS
>DIRECT LABOR PER DOLLAR PRODUCED
>EXCESS FREIGHT
>UNPLANNED OVERTIME, DOWNTIME
>WAREHOUSE EXPENSE
>TAXES
>RECORD ERRORS

Figure 4. Measures of potential manufacturing control benefits.

inventory planning and production control have more credibility. A list of useful measures is given in Fig. 4.

Most of these are self-explanatory, but a few should be amplified. The inventory input-output measure is illustrated in Fig. 5. Separate sections cover purchased material versus plan, direct labor versus budget, shipments (or incoming orders) versus forecasts, and inventories versus budget. The report lists measures of inputs and outputs to inventory and tracks progress on meeting plans for each of these major factors. Such a report is necessary if companies are to achieve budgets consistently. Companies which have such controls normally hit budgets.

An effective way to measure record errors is indicated in Fig. 6. This shows the number of stocked items cycle-counted each day, indicating the percentage of items which have a "significant" error. Significance relates to the way counts are normally obtained and the value of the item. A $500 electric motor would have a significant error of plus or minus 0. An item customarily scale counted would carry a significance limit of plus or minus 2 percent. Within these acceptable limits errors would not be counted. Actual errors are tabulated in a distribution indicating how severe the problems are. The objective, of course, should be to reduce the percentage of items with significant errors toward zero and to move the error percentages toward the left into low-range columns.

Some real success stories have been documented. Black & Decker Manufacturing Company estimated recently they would have $9 million more inventory if they still ordered materials the way they did prior to improving their control system. They recently reduced work-in-process 21 percent at the same time plant output

INVENTORY INPUT-OUTPUT

MONTH	PURCH. MATL.			PROD. LABOR			SHIPMENTS			INVENTORY		
	P	A	+(-)	P	A	+(-)	P	A	+(-)	P	A	+(-)
JAN	405	438	33	322	220	(102)	1405	1329	(76)	15.6	15.3	(.3)
FEB	560	632	105	328	375	(55)	1389	1517	52	15.7	15.4	(.3)
MAR												
APR												

Figure 5.

RECORD ERRORS

DATE	ITEMS COUNTED	% ITEMS WITH SIGNIF. ERROR	% ERRORS			
			0-5	5-10	10-25	OVER 25
2-18	126	18	4	5	6	3
2-19	133	22	6	4	9	2
2-20	119	20	5	4	6	5

Figure 6. A log for recording errors.

was being increased by 16 percent. Bendix Brake and Steering Division improved inventory turnover from 4.9 to 7.0 and identified $100,000 savings in premium transportation charges over a 2 year period. Davis Manufacturing Company made a 20 percent reduction in inventories with vastly improved customer service and much smoother manufacturing operations. Ivan Sorvall reduced inventories over 20 percent in less than 1 year, while customer service percentages improved from the mid-60s to the mid-90s. Dodge Manufacturing Division of Reliance Electric handled a 25 percent increase in sales on over 8,000 stocked items, maintaining customer service above 90 percent. The literature of production and inventory management is seeing an increasing number of such testimonials to the benefits of improved control.

There are still problems to be solved by even such successful companies. However, these problems are of much greater significance than the usual crises faced by those whose systems are out of control and who depend upon informal expediting approaches to get the product to their customers on time. The benefits are tangible and can be literally enormous.

It should not be assumed, however, that benefits are achieved simply by having a good system. This is necessary, but by no means sufficient. Real gains are made only when capable managers use the system data to make better decisions and take action more promptly. The investment of time, money, and people in improving control of manufacturing operations is the only approach which improves return on investment by simultaneously increasing profits and reducing the capital required to earn them. What better investment can you make?

Making Sure You Really Get a Payoff from Your Manufacturing System

Kenneth D. Allen

President, Microline Corporation
Santa Ana, California

We who are interested not in hiding fat but in getting rid of it, know that our country, once again, is in transition. Some of the periods of major change for industry in the U.S. have been the era of the Montgomery Ward catalog and mail distribution, Henry Ford's automobile and mass production, and jet aircraft, computers, and high technology. The 1970's are forecast as the age of productivity, and it will be a unique era of its own.

Competition on the international scene will be an increasingly strong factor and will dramatically affect our way of doing business. The European Common Market is rapidly emerging as an economic block joining the Japanese as a powerful competitive force. The Japanese will continue to apply themselves aggressively with great ingenuity. For instance, the Toyota assembly line does not maintain a stockroom. It is scheduled on a minute-to-minute basis. With Toyota's vendors operating as satellite companies, operations are scheduled to serve Toyota's assembly line on a minute-to-minute basis. Last year the Japanese purchased major quantities of lumber from the U.S. The lumber was converted into cabinets on a manufacturing ship prior to its arrival in Japan. These are examples of creative manufacturing leading to high productivity. Increasing our productivity will be essential to our economic survival in the future.

Dynamics and Manufacturing

Manufacturing has always been a dynamic environment. In the 1970's it is expected to be a raging battlefield. In the past, Marketing and Engineering have been able to operate with relatively high independence from the Manufacturing operation. It was not necessary for the sales force to understand how the product was manufactured. We manufacturing people have oftentimes assumed the responsibility for

DYNAMICS

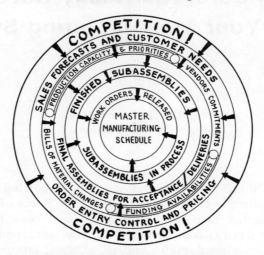

MANUFACTURING

Figure 1.

converting an engineering prototype into a producible product. In other words, the engineers were also not conscious of the manufacturing process.

The challenge for Manufacturing in the future will be the integration of all those operations into a system that is highly producible. Competitive pressures converge on the master manufacturing schedule, as shown in Fig. 1. The manufacturing system must be responsive and adaptive to this dynamic environment. How is the master schedule effected? What should be purchased and produced?

Happiness

One of the most dynamic people I know was the Vice President of Operations at Microdata Corporation, a manufacturer of mini-computers. He introduced me to a slogan, "Happiness is shipping on schedule." It has been my experience that the master schedule often dominates the priorities of the manufacturing operation. The philosophy of the manufacturing man tends to be, "Come hell or high water we are going to meet this month's shipping schedule." Sometimes this also means excess inventory investment, which naturally leads to obsolescence and inventory writeoffs.

```
┌─────────────────┐
│                 │
│  HAPPINESS  IS  │
│  SHIPPING  ON   │
│  SCHEDULE       │
│                 │
│                 │
└─────────────────┘
```

Figure 2.   PRIORITIES . . ???

The Manufacturing Manager is frequently characterized as a fire-breathing monster. Since many of these people are well organized, highly intelligent, and dynamic, I interpret their stormy nature to be the outgrowth of a frustrating environment, the source of these frustrations being inadequate tools to do the job. The answer to relieving this frustration may be a manufacturing management system (Fig. 2) which provides a method for being responsive to the company's priorities.

Who Should Be Responsible for the Payoff To Be Derived
from the Manufacturing *Management System*?

Implementing these systems is clearly a team effort (see Fig. 3). The President has the ultimate responsibility for goal setting and profit performance. The Marketing Manager must determine customer needs, the competition, and what is needed to *win*. The Engineering Department designs the winning product. Manufacturing must produce a quality product on a timely basis with maximum inventory turn and minimum obsolescence. The best Sales Department cannot be successful without a good Manufacturing Department, and vice versa, the best Manufacturing Department cannot be successful unless the Sales Department is providing orders.

Business Planning

Business planning (Fig. 4) is the key to the successful implementation of a manufacturing management system. It provides the basis for obtaining commitment to achieve payoff and for measuring progress toward these payoffs. The actual commitment can be divided into two areas: system implementation and system operation. An outline of the business plan is summarized below.

Overall Performance Objectives. This includes basic marketing strategy and 5-year sales/profit goals.

Competition. An accurate assessment of the competition is extremely important. This can be obtained by reviewing competitors' annual reports, Dunn & Bradstreet reports, and product literature. One of the best sources of information about your competitors is calling their salesmen directly. Normally, they won't even ask who you are. Just ask them how they beat your company, why their products are better than yours, and what they quote in the way of price and delivery. Better yet, call your own salesman—sometimes you may find him being overly optimistic about the promises they make to customers. They may be making commitments to which your company cannot perform, which over the long pull is bad business practice.

Product Analysis. Where are you today and where are you going? We will return to this subject later.

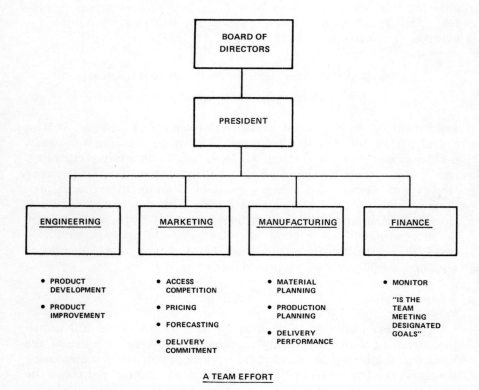

Figure 3. A team effort.

Current Management Control System. The current system should be flowcharted. This will illuminate those areas where the system breaks down and interferes with maximizing your performance.

The Tradeoff Analysis/Alternate Systems. Selection of a system alternative is dependent upon the payoff potential for the organization. The alternatives frequently break down into three types of systems:

· Manual or service bureau

· Batch computer systems

· Communications-oriented Production and Inventory Control System

BUSINESS PLANNING

● **OVERALL PERFORMANCES OBJECTIVES**

● **COMPETITION**

● **PRODUCT ANALYSIS**

● **INVENTORY ANALYSIS**

● **CURRENT MANUFACTURER'S MANAGEMENT CONTROL SYSTEM**

● **TRADE-OFF ANALYSIS — ALTERNATE SYSTEMS**

● **IMPLEMENTATION PLAN**

● **PAYOFF (JUSTIFICATION)**

Figure 4.

Implementation Plan. As your planning proceeds, the best system approach becomes clear. The overall system design extends into more detailed design where the implementation schedule and cost can be precisely defined. The implementation of the system should usually be evolutionary where benefits from the operation of the system are established in the early phases. The data base is built in modular fashion; the reports to be generated from the system are also generated from the data base and evolve into a comprehensive reporting and control system.

Payoff. The payoff for implementing and operating the system constitutes the basis for justification of the overall plan. This justification should be related to the profit and loss statement and invested assets.

The business plan is the key to obtaining commitment from the management team. It should represent the principles of management by objective. A discussion of the product and inventory analysis should better illustrate this point.

Product and Inventory Analysis

Figure 5 breaks down the financial goals of the business by product line.

Delivery Requirement. In order to determine the level of inventory investment required to support a particular product line, the Marketing Department should define delivery requirements. These requirements can normally be stated in terms of a certain percentage of the product line to be delivered off the shelf and a certain

PRODUCT LINE	DELIVERY REQUIREMENT		INVENTORY			EXCESS INVENTORY	SALES	COST	GROSS PROFIT	INVENTORY
			RAW	W.I.P.	FINISHED GOODS					
2100	SHELF	35%	653,000	459,000	1,247,000	603,000	12,256,000	6,105,000	50%	2.0
	15 DAYS	20%								
	30 DAYS	20%								
3000	SHELF	20%	445,000	406,000	789,000	150,000	14,796,000	5,980,000	59%	3.3
	15 DAYS	30%								
	30 DAYS	50%								
			1,098,000	865,000	2,036,000	753,000	27,052,000	12,085,000	55%	2.5

COMMIT THE TEAM TO MEASURABLE, TANGIBLE GOALS

Figure 5. Commit the team to measurable, tangible goals.

percentage of the product line delivered in terms of days or months. The Marketing Department can support this analysis by analyzing their volume of quotations, capture ratio, the delivery commitments being promised customers, and the performance of the company in delivering to these companies on a timely basis. What percentage of the commitments are past due? A comparison of the data with the competitor's performance should allow a precise definition of the desired delivery goals for the company.

Inventory Requirements. Marketing normally presents a forecast of projected sales for a product line. The analysis of sales versus delivery requirements should determine the level of finished goods inventory that should be maintained in support of each product line. The determinations of inventory levels for raw material and work in process in support of a product line is not always straightforward. In other words, the company may not always have a satisfactory manufacturing control system for computing this information. In an assembled product manufacturing company it is all but impossible to relate raw material and work in process performance to the sales forecast which is normally in terms of end item part numbers. The computation of raw material and work in process may be dependent upon a material requirements planning system.

However, raw material and work in progress inventory can be estimated based upon the manufacturing time required to assemble products and management's best estimate of the level of raw materials required and current vendor performance.

A company frequently finds a major difference between the estimated inventory levels required to support a product line and the actual inventory levels currently maintained.

The table shown in Fig. 5 is estimated and compared with the actual inventory and current manufacturing control system. The area where the system breaks down should be clearly illuminated. This analysis is the foundation for determining where you are today and, in the management team's judgment, a plan for achieving an improved set of goals. In this manner the team can be committed to measurable, tangible goals.

The Tradeoff Analysis. Figure 6 is a manufacturing control system overview. A comprehensive system should be designed which supports the company's 5-year objectives. After the overall system and the reporting requirements are clearly defined, the creation of the data base can be scheduled (Fig. 7). Similarly, report availability (Fig. 8) dates can be scheduled. These schedules should allow for evolution. For example, an on-line inventory inquiry system can be installed and allowed to operate in parallel with the manual inven-

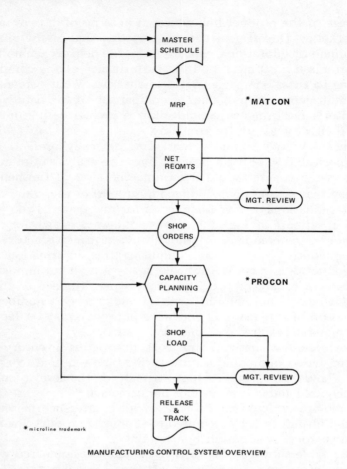

MANUFACTURING CONTROL SYSTEM OVERVIEW

Figure 6. Manufacturing control system overview.

tory record system. The use of the computerized inventory record system should allow for convenient posting and updating of the manual system as these systems operate in parallel.

The bills of material are established; where-used processing provides an in-depth analysis of the current inventory record system. This results in a precise determination of invalid part numbers, inactive stock, and active stock. The next step may be to generate kit availability reports to minimize the pulling and staging of incomplete kits until complete material is delivered to the stockroom. In this case, the overall system is planned to evolve from a computer based

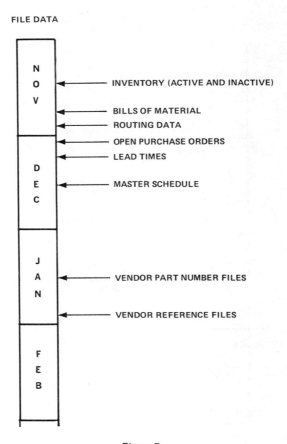

Figure 7.

"Kardex file," providing minimal but immediate operating benefits into a comprehensive manufacturing and control system, including time-phased net requirements, shop loading, and work in process tracking. It is important that this progress toward this implementation schedule be closely monitored. If the major milestones are not adhered to, the project oftentimes flounders. I am aware of a number of companies who have invested hundreds of thousands of dollars in implementing systems of this type only to scrap the project. This is a major expenditure and loss for a company whose annual sales are in the $15 million range.

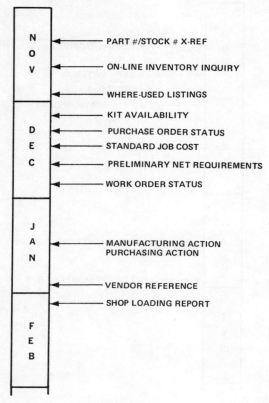

Figure 8.

Where Do People Get Clobbered in these Projects?
How Do You Avoid the Pitfalls and Reap the Benefits?

Figure 9 enumerates the typical system methodology pitfalls.

Reaction Time. Manufacturing is a dynamic environment. Systems without adequate response make it impractical to maintain an accurate data base or to provide reports on a timely basis.

People. There are major "people" problems in many computerized systems. The source of this difficulty is oftentimes lack of understanding. The systems may be much too complex and difficult to use.

SYSTEM METHODOLOGY PITFALLS

- REACTION TIME

- PEOPLE

- FILE ACCURACY

- FILE ACCESSIBILITY

- SYSTEM COMPLEXITY

- PROGRAMMING

Figure 9.

Figure 10.

Figure 11.

File Accuracy. Inaccurate files cause people to lose confidence and revert to dependence on informal systems.

File Access. In this dynamic environment, people may not be able to wait 5 days for the processing of month-end accounting reports. It may be essential to use the computer for editing rapidly changing files such as bills of material and inventory transaction postings.

Figure 10 depicts the importance of interdepartmental relationships. As pointed out in *Fortune* magazine, "It was one thing to computerize payrolls, an area that involves just one company department. It's quite another to try to computerize all, or almost all, company operations." "This can cost money and bloodshed," says Frederic G. Withington, a computer-industry analyst with Arthur D. Little, Inc. "The software to do it efficiently and quickly does not exist."*

These systems have to be easier to use. At Microline Corporation we have coined the term "player piano simplicity." With the modern video display terminal, computers can be easier to use than a player piano. As one user pointed out, "You don't even have to use your feet."

Figure 11 shows a dedicated mini-computer-based terminal oriented system. Powerful, low cost, reliable, high performance hardware is now available. The architecture of these systems should

* Bylinsky, Gene, "IBM's Toughest Competitor is—IBM." *Fortune*, March 1972, p. 145.

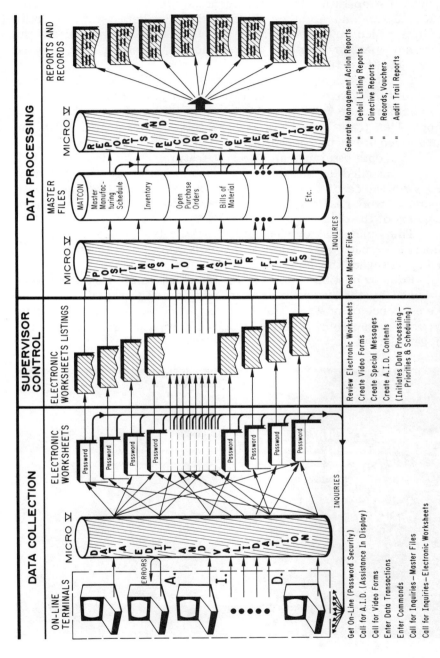

Figure 12. Data assurance architecture.

provide for operation by nonprofessional personnel while preserving file integrity and accuracy. Figure 12 shows data assurance architecture which supports these goals. This architecture isolates the terminal operator from the master files so that data is not posted directly to these files.

In this particular system, multiple users have simultaneous access to the system. Each department can have personnel entering transaction data into the system on a noninterference basis. The input files (called electronic worksheets) are protected from unauthorized access by passwords.

This data assurance architecture features source data collection. Data is installed in the system by personnel who are fully aware of the significance of the data, rather than an intermediate keypunch operator who has absolutely no knowledge of the real source or meaning of the data.

The input files or electronic worksheets can be examined by supervisory personnel at the source collection point prior to authorizing posting of the data to the master files.

Prior to posting to the master files, these input files can also be reviewed by the system supervisor, can be listed as audit trails, and the sequence of posting established by supervisor control. This data assurance architecture protects the user from the barrels of "garbage in, garbage out."

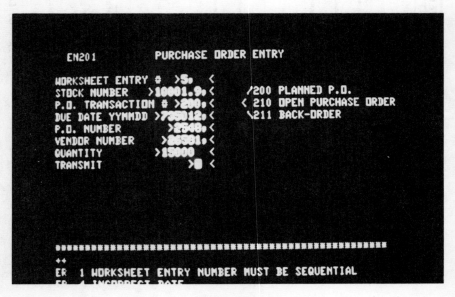

Figure 13.

The computer terminal is a boon to source data collection. It overcomes many of the problems associated with keypunch and punch cards. Many users report that on the average there is one keystroke error per 200 keystrokes.

The terminal permits the user to edit the data in the context of a form. Figure 13 shows a purchase order entry form on a video display terminal. After the terminal operator edits the input data record, the record is transferred to the computer where it performs on-line validation. If the data record does not pass certain validation procedures, error messages are transmitted back to the terminal demanding that the operator correct the input record before proceeding to the next task. The source data collection permits the user to assign accountability for the accuracy of input transactions in files. It eliminates the uncertainties caused by having an intermediate activity (such as a keypunch operation) responsible for data accuracy.

Figure 14 shows the use of a video display terminal for displaying inventory status on a single item. In this case, the availability of chip capacitors is being displayed, including 3 voltage levels (50V, 100V, and 200V) and 3 tolerance levels (5 percent, 10 percent, and 20 percent). This permits the company to decide upon alternate inventory which could satisfy a particular customer.

Companies may have tens of thousands of inventory items. It may be impossible to do a complete stock status listing on a daily or

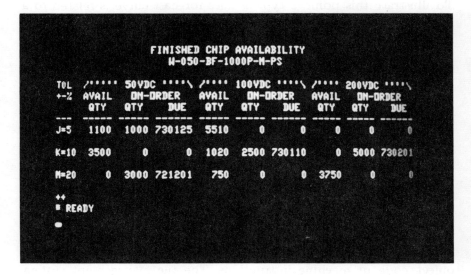

Figure 14.

weekly basis. The on-line access to a specific item can be critical to large payoff applications, particularly in support of order entry.

Time Is Money

Figure 15 shows the relationship of response time to alternate systems approaches. The data collection process for the batch system versus the communications-oriented system is significantly slower. For instance, in the batch system inventory transactions must be logged, forwarded to the keypunch room, keypunched, computer scheduled for edit run, return of error listings to the source, correction of error listings, rekeypunched, etc. In the case of the communications-oriented system, these transactions can be installed in the computer in a much shorter period of time, and the responsibility for the accuracy for these inputs can be clearly assigned.

The time to communicate answers for the batch computer system versus communications-oriented system is also significantly less. The batch system tends to produce bulk reports to cover all possible requirements. In contrast, the communications-oriented system generates exception reports. An example of this is on-line inquiry whereby the stock status or inventory availability can be ascertained on-line, eliminating the need for batch reporting of stock status.

Figure 16 relates business risk to alternate system approaches. To illustrate this point, a typical sales forecast curve is related to a backlog curve. As the forecast extends in time, the difference between the backlog curve and the forecast curve represents a probability of forecast error. It is proportional to business risk either in terms of the inventory investment or unavailability of inventory to support a production need, etc. The more responsive the system, the longer decisions can be deferred and the less exposure there is to business risk. Therefore, time is of the essence.

The communications-oriented system featuring terminals has a clear advantage over batch-oriented systems. These systems are available, but a word of caution to the user planning to install such a system is in order. Although the communications-oriented system will support "player piano simplicity" at the terminal, the internal organization of the system involves complex operating systems and application programs. Figure 17 illustrates a manufacturing management control system which has been implemented on a mini-computer. The disc operating system represents 300,000 words of object code or machine instructions. The file management system represents an additional 100,000 words, the material control system

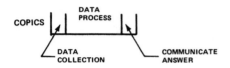

Figure 15. Alternate systems vs. time.

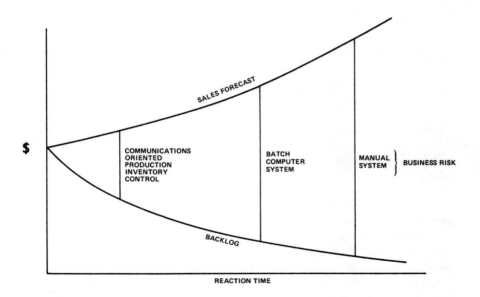

Figure 16. "Time is of the essence."

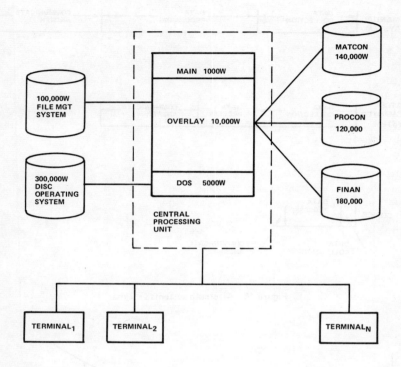

Figure 17. Communications-oriented system.

140,000 words, the production control system 120,000 words, and the financial reporting system 180,000 words. In order to conserve main memory, the system overlays program segments stored on disc into a core memory.

In order to preserve system flexibility and maintainability, it is important that a system of this capability be implemented in a high-level language. The reprogramming and maintenance of a complex system of this magnitude is impractical at the assembly language level. The user should select with care the programming language in which the system is to be implemented, maintained, and documented. The user should use established field proven software as the foundation for his system.

Summary

In summary, the manufacturing environment is dynamic and time critical. The implementation of a manufacturer's management control system is a team effort. Comprehensive business planning is essential to defining the payoff goals, to obtaining commitment, and to measuring progress toward these goals. These goals should be measurable and tangible and directly related to asset investment and profit and loss inventory turn. These systems have enormous payoff potential. They involve the integration of a number of departments and overall company operations. This project should be accomplished with professionals who can accommodate the complexity of computer programming with the dynamics of a manufacturer's operation.

The turnkeying of systems of this type will become a widespread practice. Measurex is a company installing complex systems which control the manufacturing process. Measurex offers a money-back guarantee on system performance, a factor which should have enormous appeal to many companies.